LIVING FAITH

LIVING FAITH

KEEPING *your* TESTIMONY *in* FOCUS

VINCENT ANDERSON

CFI
An imprint of Cedar Fort, Inc.
Springville, Utah

ISBN 13: 978-1-4621-2130-4

Published by CFI, an imprint of Cedar Fort, Inc.
2373 W. 700 S., Springville, UT 84663
Distributed by Cedar Fort, Inc., www.cedarfort.com

LIBRARY OF CONGRESS CATALOGING-IN-PUBLICATION DATA

Names: Anderson, Vincent, 1974- author.
Title: Living faith : keeping your testimony in focus / Vincent Anderson.
Description: Springville, Utah : CFI, An imprint of Cedar Fort, Inc., [2017] | Includes bibliographical references and index.
Identifiers: LCCN 2017045923 (print) | LCCN 2017053613 (ebook) | ISBN 9781462128532 (epub, pdf, mobi) | ISBN 9781462121304 (perfect bound : alk. paper)
Subjects: LCSH: Faith. | Christian life--Mormon authors. | Witness bearing (Christianity)--Church of Jesus Christ of Latter-day Saints. | Mormon Church--Doctrines. | Church of Jesus Christ of Latter-day Saints--Doctrines.
Classification: LCC BX8656 (ebook) | LCC BX8656 .A5235 2017 (print) | DDC 248.4/89332--dc23
LC record available at https://lccn.loc.gov/2017045923

Cover design by Shawnda T. Craig

Edited by Kathryn Watkins and Kaitlin Barwick
Typeset by Kaitlin Barwick

Printed in the United States of America

10 9 8 7 6 5 4 3 2 1

Printed on acid-free paper

Praise for LIVING FAITH

Though faith has always come naturally in my experience, I've felt some difficulty explaining it to my children or to my non-member husband or friends who don't employ the same faith application. These conversations have since been enriched by *Living Faith*. *Living Faith* provides incredible training in the mechanics of faith and gives beautiful language and scriptural back story to application. The profound insights presented add depth to the scripture stories and deepen my understanding not only of the mechanics but also the empowering application of faith. I have used the lessons countless times as foundation to many Primary, temple prep, and Relief Society lessons as well as in casual life conversations. I will be regularly revisit this book as a tool for further study and deeper awareness of my own faith practice.

—Liberty Naegle

I really believe this is an inspired work. This book contains simple, applicable, and powerful lessons on faith. Truly, a tremendous "how to" manual on a foundational gospel principle.

—Richard Dean

CONTENTS

CONTENTS

PREFACE

I DIDN'T START OFF WRITING A BOOK, ESPECIALLY NOT ON A subject as profound and important as faith. What's written here started off as a series of lessons to young teenagers—a group of Young Men I taught at church. I felt as if the lessons were inspired, and I learned a great deal while preparing them. I then began to recognize that a lot of people were discussing issues in their lives related to various things I had been addressing in those lessons, and I felt compelled to get my notes down. I thought if I did that, I might be able to share some of what I had learned. So I started off intending to write an essay that could serve as a guide to the series of lessons and allow the reader to experience them one by one as they were originally set out.

Well, after several months into the writing process, I found my essay wasn't finished, and the page count kept getting higher. One day I realized I was unintentionally writing a book. What originally started off as the simple basics suddenly tied in with many questions I had pondered for a long time and which I heard other people questioning. I continued to feel that I received further inspiration as more thoughts built on what I had already written, and I was compelled to keep writing. The individual lessons expanded into sections of the book, and a flow developed among the sections. Not only do the sections flow into each other but they also build on each other as the book goes on. Many of the concepts presented at the beginning are tied together with those at the end. I feel that I have gained further understanding of the principles discussed, and also that I have written many things that did not come from me.

Please don't think either I or this book represents some sort of "authority" on faith—because that is not how I feel. I feel like the book is an invitation to study, and I keep learning new things each time I study the principles discussed in here. There are many who have spoken very powerfully on the subject of faith, and I am sure many more will offer insights and powerful testimonies of the principles of faith. That being said, this work is meant to represent an exploration or a journey through study and learning more than a recitation of authority. I hope your experience can be similar to mine in that by learning and reviewing the things written here, you may open your mind to see faith a little clearer and open your heart to feel faith a little deeper. My goal from the beginning has simply been to offer some of the insights I have experienced to help you, the reader, progress along your personal journey of life with faith as an active principle.

I don't think of this book as a "one pass through" sort of work. You will see as you start to read it that it cycles back on itself and builds. Thus, I would encourage the reader to simply go through the whole book to start the process of pondering and feeling, and then go back through the areas or principles that you feel you would like to learn more about. More than anything, I hope this inspires you to feel something and inspires you to study and pray and live a little better so you come closer to Jesus Christ.

My goal was to write something that would be understandable to children but insightful for an adult. I wanted something to introduce the basic concepts of faith to the young but also something to prompt thoughts that would challenge the more experienced. I would love for your mind to expand as you think about things in new ways and hopefully feel the promptings of the Holy Spirit teaching you. I have children of my own that I hope will read this book and try to live by these principles. I hope the same principles will be accepted and lived by others as well.

I expect that many readers, like me, enjoy taking notes, making comments, or otherwise recording their thoughts when reading the type of subject matter this book is about. For that reason, I have tried to provide margins large enough to accommodate reader notes. I encourage you to use the margins for your own thoughts and insights. Add your own stories and thoughts to my stories and the accounts of the scriptures presented in here. Ultimately, scripture teaches us that the Holy Spirit is the real teacher (see D&C 42:14–17), so these words will be unlikely to make any difference to the reader without God's Spirit touching your soul as you read them.

I suppose I should also share my persuasion at the outset. I am an active member of the Church of Jesus Christ of Latter-day Saints, and my writing reflects faith in both the Bible and modern scripture as a companion to the Bible. All thoughts in this book belong to me, and I do not speak for the Church or for anyone whose works I quote. Think of it as an invitation to discover rather than an expounding on "doctrine." With that understanding, I hope the Spirit will inspire you and cause your faith and testimony to expand as you read these words.

A Word to the Reader

Faith is the first principle of the Gospel of Jesus Christ (see Articles of Faith 4). Without faith, it is impossible to please God (see Hebrews 11:6). And yet, I have found throughout my life that faith does not come easily to me. Perhaps it is because I am an academic thinker. Perhaps faith is a spiritual gift that I do not come by naturally, and so I will have to work to lay hold of it.

I have read a lot on faith that is theoretical and academic, and while those readings have provided great information, it seems I was missing something related to actually exercising greater faith. I hope this book will provide both an understanding and a motivation to help the reader exercise true faith. In short, I hope this is a practical tool that can help people young and older to develop and exercise faith.

I have tried to call out some of the principles of faith in this book, and to do so in a specific order based on principles I think are taught in the selected stories. However, if you read through once and then read through again, you will see how the teachings of each of the stories are interrelated.

This book is divided into topics that discuss a principle of faith. Many of the principles are discussed with reference to various analogies or exercises. If I were giving a lesson to a class, these analogies and exercises would be in the form of object lessons. Most object lessons will start by having you think about something other than faith. My goal is to begin this way to open your mind so you will be ready to entertain new ideas. Once you are at that point, I believe you will be ready to learn something new, even when we are looking at things you may have already looked at and considered. So take the time to slowly go through the analogies as you read, since I think it increases the value of the rest of what is written.

Likewise, I address a number of verses of scripture in this book, many of which you may have already read and pondered. Please understand that my purpose is not to tell you *what* to think about these verses but to provide an exercise in *how* to think about these verses. Even though you will have seen many of these verses before, keep your mind open to look at the same verse in different ways, which will allow you to learn new things from the same material. In fact, we will go through the same verses multiple times in this book, looking at them in different ways. Repetition helps us commit understanding to our hearts and provides us an opportunity to think past what we already think we know to obtain new understanding. So whatever care you may give to going through the analogies, please make sure to give even more careful attention to the scriptures, and you will understand far more than what I am able to communicate in the following pages. Let this book encourage your personal study of the scriptures.

VISION *of* FAITH

IMAGINE I WROTE THE WORD *FAITH* ON ONE PIECE OF PAPER, and the word *doubt* on another. Now imagine you place the word *faith* away from you, and keep the word *doubt* close to you. If you tried to read the words, you would notice that your vision won't allow you to focus on both the word *doubt* and the word *faith* at the same time. One has to go out of focus for you to bring the other into focus; you cannot ever focus on both at the same time. For faith to become clear, you will have to stop focusing on the doubt right in front of you, and choose to look out. In our lives, it seems that doubt is frequently right in front of us, while faith is something we have to look up to see. The Vision of Faith is about learning to focus on faith and looking past our doubts.

Let's take a look at a story from the beginning of the Book of Mormon. This story, like all scripture stories we'll review, keeps teaching us more the more we study it. In 1 Nephi, the prophet Lehi sends his sons to get a set of brass plates from Laban, who was steward over the plates. These plates contained a record of their genealogy and history. The older sons, Laman and Lemuel, complain about having to go. The younger son, Nephi, goes willingly. Their reactions can teach us a lot about faith and doubt and the Focus of Faith.

We learn from 1 Nephi 2 that the older brothers "did murmur in many things against their father. And thus Laman and Lemuel, being the eldest, did murmur against their father. And they did murmur because they knew not the dealings of that God who had created them" (1 Nephi 2:11–12). Contrast Laman and Lemuel's response with Nephi's response in 1 Nephi 3:7, "And it came to pass that I, Nephi, said unto my father: I will go and do the things which the Lord hath commanded, for I know that the Lord giveth no commandments unto the children of men, save he shall prepare a way for them that they may accomplish the thing which he commandeth them." So do we just decide that Laman and Lemuel complain because they have no faith, and Nephi obeys because he has faith, or is there some other way to understand this?

Notice that Laman and Lemuel murmured or complained when asked to do something hard *because they did not understand how God deals with His children*. Nephi obeyed willingly specifically because he knew how the Lord deals with His children. More specifically, Nephi knows the Lord prepares the way for all things He asks us to do. Maybe that's a clue about where our exercise of faith starts. Nephi's knowledge or understanding, and Laman and Lemuel's lack of understanding, appear to be important to the exercise of faith. In fact, this understanding is key to our Vision of Faith. Understanding how God deals with His children will help us lift our gaze from the doubt right in front of us to see faith down the road. Laman and Lemuel saw nothing but doubt and fear, while Nephi saw faith because he knew God would prepare the way for him to accomplish what the Lord had asked them to do.

We see this even more as we continue with their story. In 1 Nephi 3, we learn that Nephi and his brothers make two failed attempts to get the plates. Failed attempt number one is when the brothers "cast lots," or use chance, to see who gets to go ask Laban for the plates (Laman was the lucky one). Laban doesn't want to give them up in response to a polite request, accuses Laman of being a thief, and chases him out threatening to kill him (see 1 Nephi 3:11). Laman's reaction to the experience is essentially to say, "We tried, let's go home" (see 1 Nephi 3:12).

Here is the first time we see that Nephi's understanding gives him a completely different vision—the Vision of Faith. While Laman is ready to give up and go home, Nephi's reaction is this: "As the Lord liveth, and as we live, we will not go down unto our father in the wilderness until we have accomplished the thing which the Lord hath commanded us. Wherefore, let us be faithful in keeping the commandments of the Lord" (1 Nephi 3:15–16). Despite any doubt that might have come up by knowing the guy he's supposed to get the plates from now wants to kill him, Nephi is able to trust that the Lord prepares a way. Like Nephi, with the Vision of Faith, we don't focus on the doubt caused by the circumstances that surround us, but we trust in our faith that the Lord prepares a way for us to keep His commandments. Notice that Nephi tells his brothers that "as the Lord liveth, and as we live," Nephi was going to be faithful to God's commandments. I find it interesting that he entrusted his own life and honor on the faith that God lives and would come through for him. The phrase "as the Lord liveth, and as we live" has the format of an old Hebrew oath, "the one oath that no man would dream of breaking, the most solemn of all oaths to the Semite."[1] When we can see with that kind of vision, we cannot be held back by doubt, and will find a way to keep each command God gives us.

With that renewal of faith, the brothers try again, this time with a plan. Failed attempt number two is when the brothers attempt to purchase the plates from Laban. They gather the valuables in their abandoned home and return to offer them to Laban in exchange for the plates. Laban decides he will keep their property without giving them the plates (interesting for someone so willing to call someone else a thief). They again run for their lives from the servants of Laban (see 1 Nephi 3:16–27). Try to place yourself in their situation and imagine the frustration and discouragement they must have felt. They knew they were supposed to get the plates, but their ideas didn't work. After ending in failure twice, Laman and Lemuel took out their frustration on Nephi and other younger brother Sam with a stick.

Before we get too heavy on the criticism of Laman and Lemuel, let's consider what they were thinking here—to see with their vision, if you will; the vision without faith. Consider the feelings of frustration and doubt you have felt when the thing you are trying to accomplish doesn't appear to go well. I'll admit that my natural tendency is to get frustrated more quickly than I should. Maybe many of us wouldn't have grabbed a stick and joined Laman and Lemuel, but ask yourself honestly if you are more likely to be like Nephi or Laman and Lemuel in this situation. How do you deal with the feelings of frustration of expectations missed, of your best plans failing, and really wanting to destroy something?

Their story takes an interesting twist, as an angel comes to restrain their violence. The angel then tells the brothers to go again and that "the Lord will deliver Laban into your hands"

(1 Nephi 3:29–30). The next verse reveals as much about the Vision of Faith as the initial responses by Nephi and Laman and Lemuel. First we're told how Laman and Lemuel react: "And after the angel had departed, Laman and Lemuel again began to murmur, saying: How is it possible that the Lord will deliver Laban into our hands? Behold, he is a mighty man, and he can command fifty, yea, even he can slay fifty; then why not us?" (1 Nephi 3:31). They still do not believe. We could probably say that they refuse to believe. They have spiritual blindness that keeps them from seeing anything but the doubts and fears that surround them. They are unwilling to consider another scenario where faith might conquer their concerns.

Again, to me it is interesting to see why they didn't believe. Let's modernize this story for a minute. Laman and Lemuel were saying that Laban was one fearsome guy. I like to think of him as the commander of a special forces unit ("he can command fifty"), and not just the commander, but someone who earned his command by being tougher than anyone else ("yea, even he can slay fifty"). All Laman and Lemuel could see was how fearsome Laban was. They had already been in his presence and had seen him command his men (as he sent his men to kill them). In their fear, nothing else could move them. All they saw was doubt. What did it matter to them that an angel had told them to go back when they were certain they were going to be killed if they did? They were fixated on what their mortal eyes could see, and what their mortal minds could understand. Notice they end their statement with "then why not us?" They did not believe that God has power over everything and everyone. They could not see how Laban could be overpowered by a God they could not see. We often see our temporal problems up close and personal. They seem insurmountable to us, and it can be incredibly frightening to hand them over to God and trust in Him. We don't have a bird's eye view or a perfect eternal perspective, so all we see is the potential for ruin.

Laman and Lemuel had already tried everything they could think of and had barely escaped with their lives. Their fear and disbelief would not permit them to even imagine that the Lord could deliver on the promise made by the angel, where he said God would deliver Laban into their hands. Their response was: "How is it possible that the Lord will deliver Laban into our hands?" (1 Nephi 3:31). Recall that they did not understand the dealings of that God who had created them. I imagine that they were the kind of individuals that found the miracles of their people (Moses and the Red Sea, or manna in the wilderness) to be fairy tales, or perhaps exaggerations, or stories in history about a God who was no longer interested in the daily lives of individuals. They refused to give any room in their hearts for the idea that God could perform a miracle if necessary to accomplish His purposes. In short, they had spiritual blindness when it came to the Vision of Faith—they could not see faith down the road, but would only see doubt right in front of them.

Contrast that with Nephi's response in 1 Nephi 4:1, "Let us go up again unto Jerusalem, and let us be faithful in keeping the commandments of the Lord; for behold he is mightier than all the earth, then why not mightier than Laban and his fifty, yea, or even than his tens of thousands?" Notice that phrase again: "let us be faithful in keeping the commandments of the Lord." Nephi does not indicate that he knows *how* the Lord is going to keep His promise, but his response shows he is sure the Lord *will* keep His promises.

Based on that certainty of understanding, Nephi became committed to do whatever he could to be faithful to what was requested of him. One of the most important parts of the Vision of Faith is to understand that the Lord has power to keep His promises. Nephi was sure that if they were faithful in keeping the commandments the Lord would deliver them. Where Laman and Lemuel saw only that Laban "can command fifty, yea, even he can slay fifty; then why not us?" Nephi saw that the Lord "is mightier than all the earth, then why not mightier than Laban and his fifty, yea, or even than his tens of thousands?" Seeing with the Vision of Faith involves opening our hearts to believe in what we have been commanded to do.

When we need greater faith, we can follow Nephi's example as explained in 1 Nephi 4. Specifically, Nephi remembered the past and the times when God had manifested His power to help those who were obeying His commandments. In verse 2, Nephi recalls God's power of deliverance to the house of Israel when Moses led them across the Red Sea. In verse 3, he recalls a promise by the angel to deliver him and his brethren. Reflecting on previous demonstrations of God's power and our own experiences where our faith was rewarded can assure us that the Lord is capable of delivering us *now*. We can act on His words because we remember that when we have been faithful and obedient in the past, the hand of the Lord took care of us. Such a vision empowers us to move forward.

I believe Nephi's remembering helped him to see again with the Vision of Faith, which caused him to say: "Let us go up; the Lord is able to deliver us, even as our fathers, and to destroy Laban, even as the Egyptians" (1 Nephi 4:3). I think opening our mind to the possibility that God has power to help us succeed is the first step of faith. By opening our mind and seeing such a vision, we can firm up our trust that God can, *and will*, provide the help we need. That gives us enough courage to act, despite any doubts we may see.

We learn that Nephi still didn't understand how the Lord would deliver him, but he understood that the Lord could, which was enough for him to act. We likewise can see with the Vision of Faith by seeing faith and seeing ourselves being obedient, even if we cannot see how God will make everything work. By focusing on the Lord's ability to keep His promises, we can lift our eyes off of the problems facing us that we would be unable to overcome ourselves, and be able to see through doubt and choose to see faith instead. We can then look down the road of faith, and rise from our fears, and get on the Lord's path.

How the Lord Deals with His Children

Based on the story above, the biggest difference between Nephi and his brothers Laman and Lemuel was their level of understanding of how the Lord deals with His children. Nephi understood, and he saw the Vision of Faith. His brothers did not understand, and they only saw doubt. So let's take a little time to discuss how the Lord deals with His children. When I was younger I used to think of God in terms of punishment and judgment. That led me to think about my relationship to God in mostly the sense of trying to be careful to not do anything wrong so I didn't get His punishments. I'm not sure why I thought that, but I've observed that many people in the Church can have this view.

I now better understand what one of my local church leaders is fond of saying: the Lord would prefer to bless us than to judge us. I've had a change in how I see the nature of God. It is true that God is a God of judgment, but I believe

He prefers mercy to judgment. When judgement is necessary, His judgments are perfect. I think the Lord uses punishment as a "last resort" and allows people to receive the natural consequences of their wrong actions when they choose disobedience to the commandments. Scripture reaffirms to us over and over again that the Lord is merciful.[2] I believe that if you are making any efforts to come unto Christ, the one thing you can count on is mercy, because God is full of mercy, patience, and love for those who seek Him. If we reject Him, we receive His judgments to lead us back to Him.

It is important to understand that sometimes bad things happen that are not punishments but life's challenges. Some of these feel "worse" than punishment. But rather than getting concerned about whether a bad thing is a punishment or one of life's challenges, we can consider either one to be a call for us to come unto God. When we respond to that call, He will show mercy and teach us what to do to receive peace in our lives. It is so important to understand that challenges and trials are not reserved only for the wicked. God even allows hard things to come upon those He loves. And He doesn't even immediately deliver us from problems when we ask for help, which may seem odd from our mortal perspective. Trials can strengthen us and purify the soul. We don't always see the bigger picture or plan that God may have for us.

How can we see the Vision of Faith when God may not always appear to hear us? Let's discuss concepts that I heard explained in a talk by S. Michael Wilcox, *The Fourth Watch*. He states that we worship a "fourth-watch God."[3] In the time of Jesus Christ, the day started at about 6:00 a.m. and was divided into twelve hours. The night was divided into four watches, each about three hours long, starting at the end of the day. Thus the fourth watch would be the last segment of the night, starting around 3:00 a.m.

Recall the experiences recounted in Matthew 14 and Mark 6 where Jesus fed the five thousand. After performing this miracle, "Jesus constrained his disciples to get into a ship, and to go before him unto the other side, while he sent the multitudes away" (Matthew 14:22). He then went into a mountain to pray while they started across the sea in the ship. As the disciples were on the sea, a storm arose, tossing the ship with waves and blowing it back with a "contrary" wind (see Matthew 14:24). In Mark 6, we read that Jesus "saw them toiling in rowing . . . and about the fourth watch of the night he cometh unto them, walking upon the sea" (Mark 6:48). It is very significant to our discussion to know that Jesus "saw them toiling." In our own lives, we also need to remember that He sees us as we "toil" against our challenges, even if, like His disciples, we are unaware He is watching.

Surely, Jesus saw the disciples toiling through the first and second watches. And yet, it was not until they were into the fourth watch that He came. He let them toil on against the wind and waves until 3:00 or 4:00 a.m.! There are many times in our lives that we will struggle for what seems like a long, dark, spiritual night, fighting against the storms of life. We may have even been sure at the beginning of our challenge that we were directed by the Lord to get into the ship that eventually led us out into the storm. At some point, we may begin to question whether we have misunderstood the Lord's directions, and we weren't supposed to be on that ship in the first place. After all, why would He direct us out into such a storm?

Despite wanting the Lord's help with life's challenges sooner, God often waits until the last moment, the moment just before we will actually be overcome, before He offers help. Consider the accounts of Joseph Smith in the Sacred Grove (see Joseph Smith—History 1:15–16) and of Elijah and the widow (see 1 Kings 17:10–16). Joseph was at the point of sinking into despair and abandoning himself to destruction before the Lord intervened. When Elijah came and asked for a morsel of bread, it was at the very time when the widow was gathering sticks so she could dress what little remained of her barrel of meal, to share a final meager supper with her son, and then submit to death. The Lord did not send Elijah the day before, and He did not intervene for Joseph until he was ready to give up.

And so it is that He frequently waits until the point where we give up hope, the point of being overcome by the trials of life, before He intervenes. Sometimes it seems that we are past the fourth watch, and yet He still hasn't come. S. Michael Wilcox indicates another principle to remember when we face this circumstance: being "tight like unto a dish."[4] For that principle we turn to Ether 2:17, which states that the barges the Jaredites built "were exceedingly tight, even that they would hold water like unto a dish; and the bottom thereof was tight like unto a dish; and the sides thereof were tight like unto a dish; and the ends thereof were peaked; and the top thereof was tight like unto a dish; and the length thereof was the length of a tree; and the door thereof, when it was shut, was tight like unto a dish." Notice how many times the verse repeats the expression "tight like unto a dish." When scriptures seem to repeat themselves, I think we have an opportunity to try to figure out what point the Lord is trying to make. I think the repetition in this verse can teach us a couple of things. First, every part of the barge was "tight like unto a dish"—not just the bottom. Our faith and testimony can also be watertight in every aspect, so that nothing will come along and cause us to spiritually take on water and sink. The second thought is related, which is that the Lord really wants us to understand that the barges were not going to sink, because every part of the barge had been made watertight. As we'll see later in the story, when we are properly prepared, no storm will overcome us.

After making the barges in accordance with the Lord's directions, the brother of Jared came back to identify problems that he saw with them. We read about the interaction between the brother of Jared and the Lord in Ether 2. The brother of Jared states: "And behold, O Lord, in them there is no light; whither shall we steer? And also we shall perish, for in them we cannot breathe, save it is the air which is in them; therefore we shall perish" (Ether 2:19). I read this as identifying three issues: no light, no way to steer, and no air. In response to the third issue, the Lord tells the brother of Jared to make holes in the top and bottom of the ships so they could let in fresh air (see Ether 2:20). In response to the first issue, the Lord tells the brother of Jared that He wants him to come up with a solution (see Ether 2:23).

In response to the second issue, the Lord states the following: "For behold, ye shall be as a whale in the midst of the sea; for the mountain waves shall dash upon you. Nevertheless, I will bring you up again out of the depths of the sea; for the winds have gone forth out of my mouth, and also the rains and the floods have I sent forth. And behold, I prepare you against these things; for ye cannot cross this great deep save I prepare you against the waves of the sea, and the winds which have gone forth, and the floods which shall come" (Ether 2:24–25). We see the fulfillment of this in Ether 6:5–9. I find verses 8 and 9 particularly interesting: "And it came to pass that the winds did never cease to blow towards the promised land while they were upon the waters; and thus they were driven forth before the wind. And they did sing praises unto the Lord; yea, the brother of Jared did sing praises unto the Lord, and he did thank and praise the Lord all the day long; and when the night came, they did not cease to praise the Lord."

Turning this account to personal application, I would suggest that we can see that there will be "mountain waves" that will crash upon our ships. Those are those times when we, like Nephi and his brothers, will see doubt all around us and have to look up for faith. Not only might the mountain waves crash on us but the winds causing those waves will go forth out of the mouth of the Lord and will never cease to blow. In those times, it can be hard to see those winds as a positive force. But we would do well to remember that the wind that blows against us relentlessly is actually taking us to the promised land, and we, like the brother of Jared, ought to "praise the Lord all the day long" for making our way swift (Ether 2:9).

The Jaredite ships were to be "as a whale in the midst of the sea," and so at times they would be submerged, and the Lord would "bring them up again out of the depths of the sea" (Ether 2:24; see also Ether 3:2). So the Lord addressed the second issue by telling the brother of Jared that they would not need to steer, because the Lord was going to do the driving. Sometimes we don't get to steer in life, but we hang on and let the Lord drive us. My dad has told me that when we want to ride with the Lord, we need to learn to let go of the wheel and let Him do the steering. I think that is what the Lord was telling the brother of Jared. We need to remember that, ultimately, we may not know where we're going, but the Lord sees our entire journey ahead of us. We need to adopt the Vision of Faith instead of focusing on doubt.

Let's discuss one more personal application of this account to our lives. I used to think that if I was overwhelmed in life, there was something wrong. Of course, it feels like something is wrong when we feel overwhelmed. But what I mean is that

I believed that when I got overwhelmed, it was evidence that I had done something wrong or not done something right. I thought that being overwhelmed should never happen, so if I was overwhelmed, I must not be following the Lord. But now I try to take comfort in seeing that there are times in our lives that we will be overwhelmed (just as the brother of Jared was submerged in the depths of the sea) as the Lord "drives" us to the promised land. Talk about needing to adopt the Vision of Faith and stop focusing on our doubts! So how do we do that?

I try to remember that like the Jaredites, the Lord will "prepare [us] against these things" (Ether 2:24). In our own lives, there will be challenges that we cannot cross "save [He prepares us] against the waves of the sea, and the winds which have gone forth, and the floods which shall come" (Ether 2:25). There are trials and troubles we will face in life that will submerge us. They will be more than we can handle on our own. There is a difference between being *overwhelmed* and being *overcome*. We may be submerged, but we will not be sunk when the Lord prepares us beforehand. He prepares us beforehand when we try to do what is right, to the best of our understanding. There are times we will be *overwhelmed*, but we can know that we are still OK because our ship is tight like unto a dish. If we were at the point of being *overcome*, the Lord would intervene. When we let the Lord steer, we will likely encounter both situations: ones where we are overwhelmed, but in a boat that is tight like unto a dish; and ones where we are about to be overcome, and the Lord comes to us on the water in the fourth watch. In both situations, we have to trust the Lord to steer and trust that He will indeed bring us again out of the depths and into the calm.

OK, so we see that sometimes God comes in the fourth watch, and sometimes He allows us to be submerged. So when is it that God is a fourth-watch God? When is it that He will tell us that our ship is tight like unto a dish? First, I'm going to repeat and expand on something I already mentioned: it is important to understand that God is not the author of every problem or trial we face. There are some trials that come to us even as we are trying to do what the Lord asks. There are other trials that the Lord sends to guide us to a different path. And all trials can help guide us to the Lord if we will turn to Him.

In "fourth-watch" circumstances, the Lord allows us to continue to "toil against" the waves because we still have strength left, and He will not come until our strength is spent. It seems to me that the trials of life's circumstances are represented by those waves that come up as we are in the ship trying to go where the Lord has directed. In life's circumstances, we need to understand that He is going to watch and wait. He will come to us when we really need His help, but He may not come until the fourth watch.

I also think that the trials of obedience and willingness to submit our will to the Lord's will are represented by winds coming forth to blow our ship to the promised land. Such circumstances are "tight like unto a dish" circumstances, where the Lord has prepared us beforehand. We need to understand our need to be humble before the Lord and learn to become submissive to the Lord as a little child (see Mosiah 3:19). This is how the Lord deals with His children—raising them up in righteousness.

In my own experience, it is difficult to know whether I need to continue to toil to build up my strength or just let go to allow the waves to pound me to where I need to end up. Sometimes it seems as though one leads into the other. Sometimes I have to look at a situation both ways and try everything I can for either case. The important points to remember, no matter how the circumstances arise, are that the Lord is watching and that He has the power to deliver us, even if it requires a miracle such as walking on water to come to our ship. The other thing to remember is that the Lord will prepare us beforehand for when we will need it. He will not let us sink. He will either come to us in our moment of despair or He will assure us that every time we are submerged, He will bring us up again. It is easy to say, and hard to live, but we never need to despair. When you feel yourself at the point of despair, pray to know God is there, and He will let you feel of His presence. Sometimes that will have to be enough to give us the Vision of Faith to just keep going until we finally find ourselves out of the storm.

Please note that "just letting go" is not a passive experience. When I refer to letting go, I don't mean doing nothing. I do not mean there is no work involved for us. In fact, I find the work more difficult in letting go than I do in continuing to toil. When I toil against the waves, the waves are typically easy to identify. And at least I think I know where I am trying to get to. When I have to just let go, I don't know where the Lord is taking me. I may be constantly changing directions. I will be overwhelmed for at least some of the time. When I toil it may be hard, but I have not yet become submerged by the mountain waves. When I must let go, I have to let go of pride, or give up my favorite sins, or change a preconception, or do some other hard thing to learn to be guided every step of the way by the Spirit (carefully read 2 Nephi 31:17–32:6). I suspect you will find the same to be true in your life.

Remember that the Vision of Faith comes as we raise our eyes and look at something besides the problems right in front of us. The understanding of these accounts in particular, and the broader understanding of how God deals with His children in general, will help us exercise our faith in these circumstances. We can be like Nephi in knowing that God prepares a way. When we trust that to be true, we will be motivated to action. We can exercise our faith a little longer, a little more, knowing that we can accomplish the things the Lord expects of us. We will pick up our eyes and look on every situation with the Vision of Faith.

Notes

1. Hugh Nibley, *An Approach to the Book of Mormon*, 2nd ed. (1964), 104–5.
2. Consider studying some of the following: Exodus 20:5–6, Nehemiah 9:16–32, Micah 7:18–19, Alma 42:14–15, and Matthew 9:10–13.
3. S. Michael Wilcox, *The Fourth Watch: Receiving Divine Help When Your Prayers Seem Unanswered*, talk on CD (Salt Lake City: Deseret Book, 2004), CD-ROM.
4. Wilcox, *The Fourth Watch.*

FOCUS *of* FAITH

Refer to the picture on the next page. It is known as a 3D autostereogram. You may be familiar with these three-dimensional illusions. The "stereo" portion refers to the fact that there are two different "channels" of information to be perceived separately by each eye. With an autostereogram, a person perceives a 3D image by staring at a 2D pattern. They work very much the same way current technology works for 3D movies and television. In current 3D technology, a scene is shot with two different camera lenses that focus on the scene from slightly different angles or slightly different perspectives. The screen displays a combination of the two different perspectives of the scene, overlapped as a single image. Those 3D glasses that you wear while watching the movie cause each eye to focus separately on the different image information. In that way, your brain will put together information received by each eye in a way that makes the two-dimensional image appear to have depth.

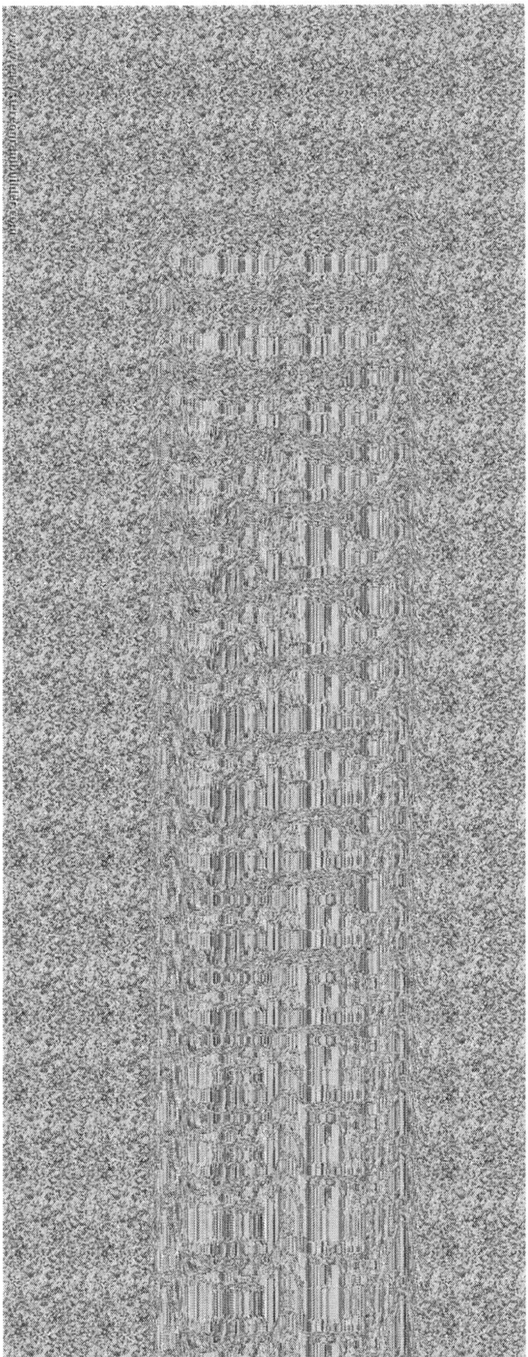

TOP

There are a couple of ways to bring autostereogram illusions into focus. The best way I know of is to hold the picture right in front of your nose (almost right against your face), and try to relax your gaze so that you look "through" the picture. Don't try to bring the picture into focus yet, and don't try to bring anything else into focus—just relax as though you are looking at something on the other side of the image. What you are trying to do is separate the stereo information for each eye separately, which is why you need it close to your face. Now slowly pull the picture away from your face while maintaining the same relaxed gaze, imagining you are seeing something through the picture. Now hold the image steady about eighteen inches in front of you and continue to hold that relaxed gaze as the picture starts to focus. You may need to move the picture back and forth toward your nose a couple of different times at first. It may take some practice, but eventually you might be able to perceive a three-dimensional effect. In the picture on the previous page, you should see a three-dimensional rendering of the word *faith*.

You will have to learn to change how you focus to be able to see the image. Exercising faith frequently also requires us to change our focus. The natural man tends to carry many biases. Such biases come with upbringing, natural tendencies and thought patterns, experiences, etc. It is very difficult to see things from any perspective but our practiced perspective. But to exercise the most powerful faith, we must be able to drop our preconceptions to make room to entertain different ideas. More specifically, we must learn to change our focus from our will to the Lord's will. It may take concerted effort and training of our spiritual sight to see the Lord's will. We may have to learn to look "through" the things we are used to seeing to open ourselves up to be able to perceive something more. There are times that people may actually see a 3D effect but not understand what the image is. Likewise, sometimes we can change our perspective enough to understand the Lord's will sufficiently to act on it but still only understand in part.

Let's talk about the Focus of Faith as having two different aspects. Both are illustrated by the activity above. First, we may need to shift our focus to be able to exercise faith. This is similar to how we train our eyes to focus differently than they normally do to perceive the autostereogram. Second, we need to maintain our focus so that we can sustain our exercise of faith and ignore those things that would cause us to doubt. This is similar to how we need to train holding our shifted focus (keeping the same gaze, as we said above) to allow the 3D image to appear.

For the first aspect, let's look at an account from Daniel 3. As pointed out by Elder Dennis E. Simmons, true faith is about much more than what we want to have happen in a given circumstance.[1] The exercise of true faith in Christ comes with an understanding that God understands all, and does what is best for all His children. We, however, understand extremely little compared to God, and usually try to do what is best for ourselves and those immediately around us, not understanding whether specific things we want are best for all of God's children. In fact, we will find that many times the things we seek are not even the best things for us. That is why we need to adopt a different perspective with the Focus of Faith to exercise true faith.

Shadrach, Meshach, and Abed-nego had been placed in positions of authority under king Nebuchadnezzar. But others jealous of their positions convinced the king to issue an edict that everyone had to worship his golden image. They then accused Shadrach, Meshach, and Abed-nego before the king, because they would only worship God and not the golden statue. Looking at Daniel 3 we read: "These men, O king, have not regarded thee: they serve not thy gods, nor worship the golden image which thou hast set up. Then Nebuchadnezzar in his rage and fury commanded to bring Shadrach, Meshach, and Abed-nego. Then they brought these men before the king. Nebuchadnezzar spake and said unto them, Is it true, O Shadrach, Meshach, and Abed-nego, do not ye serve my gods, nor worship the golden image which I have set up? Now if ye be ready [to] fall down and worship the image which I have made; well: but if ye worship not, ye shall be cast the same hour into the midst of a burning fiery furnace; and who is that God that shall deliver you out of my hands?" (Daniel 3:12–15).

So the king commands them directly to worship the golden image or he will cast them into a fiery furnace. His question to them is very interesting; he asks, "Who is that God that shall deliver you?" Such a question encourages us to see things with our natural, unchanged focus, instead of our changed Focus of Faith. Such a question is calculated to encourage doubt to make sure we do not see the things through the Focus of Faith.

Their response to the king teaches us a great deal about the Focus of Faith: "Shadrach, Meshach, and Abed-nego, answered and said to the king, O Nebuchadnezzar, we are not careful to answer thee in this matter" (Daniel 3:16). This means that they had thought through everything before giving their answer. Often the exercise of faith requires us to consider all our options, and then ask ourselves where our trust lies. They continue by explaining where they put their trust: "If it be so, our God whom we serve is able to deliver us from the burning fiery furnace, and he will deliver us out of thine hand, O king. But if not, be it known unto thee, O king, that we will not serve thy gods, nor worship the golden image which thou hast set up" (Daniel 3:17–18).

Notice that they express their confidence in the power of the Lord to deliver them ("our God whom we serve *is able* to deliver us from the burning fiery furnace") as well as their faith that He will act with that power ("and he *will deliver* us out of thine hand, O king"). But then they state: "*But if not* . . . we will not serve thy gods, nor worship the golden image which thou hast set up." The first part is how I have generally understood faith—an unwavering confidence that God will exercise His power. Notice their statement of confidence has an underlying expression of what they want to have happen (because after all, who wouldn't want to be saved?). The first statement is directed toward an understanding and trust in God's power and faithfulness to show forth His power on our behalf. The second statement is directed to an understanding of their need to be faithful no matter what happens.

When I studied these verses, James 1 came to mind: "But let him ask in faith, nothing wavering. For he that wavereth is like a wave of the sea driven with the wind and tossed. For let not that man think that he shall receive any thing of the Lord. A double minded man is unstable in all his ways" (James 1: 6–8). On the face of it, the statement "but if not" may seem to contradict the trust and confidence of the first statement. After all, first they say God will act with His power, and then they say that God might not act the way they hope. Is this wavering in their faith like James talks about? Could their expression be fairly characterized like this: "He will save us; at least I think so . . . unless He doesn't"? Is wavering what Shadrach, Meshach, and Abed-nego are doing here? I don't believe there is any wavering at all in Shadrach, Meshach, and Abed-nego, so let's work through why not.

Notice that James doesn't just say "wavering," but he also uses the expression "double minded." When I read about Shadrach, Meshach, and Abed-nego, I don't see men who were double minded. In fact, I think quite the opposite is true. See that James equates the person who wavers with a "double minded man" who "is unstable in all his ways." Maybe we can think of "double minded" as trying to look at faith and doubt at the same time, referring to the analogy in the previous section, the Vision of Faith. Someone who is double minded will see nothing more than a fuzzy, confused image. Let's go back to Shadrach, Meshach, and Abed-nego and see why they were not double minded, unstable, or wavering in their faith.

Their first statement expressed their belief and confidence that God has power and is faithful. I believe their second statement is their expression of their own faithfulness, just as God is faithful. Their second statement ("But if not, be it known unto thee, O king, that we will not serve thy gods, nor worship the golden image which thou hast set up") does not call into question God's power or faithfulness, but emphasizes their commitment to being faithful to what the Lord commands no matter the outcome. In short, they had the faith to not be saved. We have the Focus of Faith only when we overlap our commitment and faithfulness onto God's power and faithfulness. We have two channels of information to bring our faith into focus, like our autostereogram that we talked about.

Thus, to me their statement actually shows more faith, because they trust God will take care of them if they do what they are supposed to. Whether that means deliverance as they would desire, or something else that He chooses, they accept God's will over their own. When faced with the possibility of being thrown into the fire, they affirm that they will continue to do what the Lord has said, regardless of the consequences. They put their trust wholly in the Lord, being of a fixed mind rather than a double mind. They show a firm conviction that He has asked them to do something, and it is up to His will what He wants to do with them after that. Their understanding of how the Lord deals with His children is that when He asks us to do something, He wants us to do it trusting He will bless us for it. Their faith was that the Lord could provide a miracle in this life, but their understanding was that He may instead choose to bless them in the life to come.

You may know the rest of the story: They were thrown into the furnace, and the Lord saved them from the fire. They came forth out of the furnace without even being singed by the fire, or having the smell of fire on them (see Daniel 3:20–27). The Lord will not always deal with us in such a dramatic way; however, our first priority should be to always seek after the will of the Lord. When we have the Focus of Faith, we will act in faith, understanding and trusting that He will take care of us no matter the outcome.

This reminds me of times when my children have seen reports of natural disasters in the news and asked me "what if" questions. They ask about what if those bad things happened to our family. Like most parents, I find myself wanting to tell them that "everything is going to be OK," or that "I won't let anything bad happen to you." But we all know that those promises can't be true because I am not in charge. I have no power to keep those promises. But I know God has power to take care of us, and I try to see with the Focus of Faith. What I now tell my children is that I don't know if anything bad will happen in our area, and that something bad could happen to our family. I then continue by telling them, "*However*, no matter what happens, the Lord will take care of us." That much I am sure of; the Lord is faithful to take care of those who have faith in Him. Similarly, we can act in all aspects of our life with the Focus of Faith knowing that we should obey with trust in the Lord—trust that He requests our obedience, and trust that He will reward us in the way that will be best for us and all of His children.

We'll need to train both our perspective and our behavior to have the Focus of Faith necessary to exercise our faith in hard circumstances. We train our perspective by continuing to remind ourselves that the Lord knows better than we do in every situation. We can do as Nephi did, and remind ourselves of the power God has shown in the past, to remember that He does have power. When we submit ourselves to the will of God, there are some things we can be sure of. The first thing we can be sure of is about His nature and perfection. All the scripture stories teach us something of the nature of God. God is perfect in all things. He has the ability to see all things. He is merciful, and He values our agency and the agency of others. After all, life is a test, a test to see if we will seek the light in mortality that was presented to us prior to mortality (see Abraham 3:25; 4:18, 21). The second thing we can be sure of is what the Lord expects of us. There are commandments throughout the scriptures and examples of how to obey. We are supposed to come unto Him and become one with Him, by which we can turn our will to His. We need to seek after His Spirit and follow His guidance. We train our behavior by learning to obey.

As we talk about the Focus of Faith, please understand that we do not always know how the Lord will deliver on His promises. Recall that Zacharias was struck dumb because of how he acted when he couldn't see how the Lord could fulfill the promise of the angel (see Luke 1:18–20). Zacharias merely needed to do what he was asked and allow the Lord to fulfill His promises. He ran into trouble because he questioned how the Lord would carry through on His promises. He acted more like Laman and Lemuel when he should have trusted like Nephi. Similarly, while there may be benefits in envisioning ourselves carrying out each step of our personal plans, we will frequently be disappointed if we try to envision each step of the Lord's plan. The fact is that God's ways are higher than our ways (see Isaiah 55:9–11). He is able to do His own work without telling us every step of it. All we need to do is hold onto the vision of the Lord fulfilling His promises, because He always does. That is part of the Focus of Faith: we focus on the task at hand and have faith that the Lord will take care of the other steps even if we cannot see them.

So let's go back to the 3D image at the beginning of this section. Similar to how we changed our focus to "see in 3D," we change our spiritual focus and faith by submitting ourselves to the will of the Lord to see beyond our own desires. Unlike the autostereogram where we trick our minds into seeing more than what's really there, with the Focus of Faith we actually drop the illusion of our flawed personal perspective to be able to see what's really there. That is our change in perspective. We learn of God's nature, and we seek after the guidance of the Spirit. The challenge is then to put things into practice by acting on whatever the Lord asks us to do, leaving the ultimate outcome to the Lord. That is our change in behavior. The first part of the Focus of Faith is to learn to adjust our focus, knowing that the Lord knows best, and He expects us to do His will and trust the outcome to Him. Our Focus of Faith is found in seeking the Lord's will, not in acting only according to our own understanding.

Now let's talk about the second part of the Focus of Faith—maintaining our focus. For this part, let's return to the account in Matthew 14. As we think about the Focus of Faith, we must ask: what do we focus on? Recall that in the fourth watch of the night, Jesus came walking on the sea to His disciples who were struggling against the waves and wind. After toiling all night, they were about to sink, and upon seeing Jesus they thought they were seeing a spirit out on the sea. They must have considered it an ill omen, and they cried out in fear (see Matthew 14:25–26). And then we read: "But straightway Jesus spake unto them, saying, Be of good cheer; it is I; be not afraid. And Peter answered him and said, Lord, if it be thou, bid me come unto thee on the water. And he said, Come. And when Peter was come down out of the ship, he walked on the water, to go to Jesus. But when he saw the wind boisterous, he was afraid; and beginning to sink, he cried, saying, Lord, save me. And immediately Jesus stretched forth his hand, and caught him, and said unto him, O thou of little faith, wherefore didst thou doubt? And when they were come into the ship, the wind ceased" (Matthew 14:27–32).

It might be easy to see some disappointment in Peter based on this story. After all, in response to his failure to carry through, Jesus rebuked him by saying, "O thou of little faith, wherefore didst thou doubt?" But I think we'll miss some of the best teachings of this account if we don't also look at the *success* of Peter. The scriptures have accounts of many miracles that have been performed (including raising the dead), and we see them performed repeatedly throughout scripture. But in recorded history, there are only two people who have ever walked on water: Peter and the Son of God among men. Think about that for a moment: Peter accomplished something never before done, and not done since by an ordinary man! I submit that Peter's success encourages us to understand that an ordinary man displayed extraordinary faith and was able to accomplish something never done before, and never done since, as long as he maintained his focus on the Savior.

I find it hard to imagine the faith Peter must have felt to initially ask the Savior to "bid me come unto thee on the water," much less the faith required to actually jump out of the ship. Shall we again recall that this is the fourth watch of a long, stormy night? Surely Peter had toiled along with the others all night long. And yet somehow he summoned courage great enough to jump out into the stormy sea by focusing on getting out to the Savior. Then he walked on water for as long as he maintained his Focus of Faith. So I ask again, what do we focus on?

It was when Peter "saw the wind boisterous" that he became afraid and thus lost his trust, and so lost his faith. I believe it was because he lost the Focus of Faith. He knew the wind was there when he asked to come out onto the water, and he knew the wind and waves were there when he jumped out of the ship. So they didn't take him by surprise when he jumped out of the ship—he had toiled against them all night. He must have taken his focus off of Jesus and started to waver with doubt, and he became a double-minded man. His doubt told him that people do not walk on water. I imagine that he permitted doubt to allow him to question his trust that Jesus would walk with him on the water. Then he sank.

Peter did incredible things, demonstrated great faith, and in that same episode, he doubted. Where just before he had strode confidently across the waves, he sank. Sometimes, like Peter, we can forget where faith has taken us in the past. In those moments that we begin to doubt and forget where the Lord has led us safely from, we must be like Peter and call out to Him. Rather than withdraw into ourselves thinking that the Lord has abandoned us, we cry out for Him. There is so much we can do if we will train our focus on the Savior. Only when we take our focus off the Savior will the storms around us overcome us. We can seek like Peter to come unto the Lord in any circumstance, even in the storms of life. We will then be able to hear His voice through the wind and storm and know what His will is for us. As long as we focus on that, we will maintain our Focus of Faith and find that He empowers us through faith to do what we may have previously thought was impossible.

DEFINITION *of* FAITH

IMAGINE I HAVE A BAG THAT CONTAINS A NUMBER OF FAMILiar objects. I can invite you to reach into the bag to identify the items without looking at them. Your previous experience with the objects, combined with having you feel those objects will trigger your brain to identify the objects. For example, if you grasp something small and spherical, you may identify it as a small bouncy ball or a marble—and your experience with the texture and hardness of the object will allow you to tell the two apart. Similarly, you could probably identify a pen, a paperclip, a key, and many other common objects you have experience with. But some objects will be harder to identify than others, such as an animal figurine, which you may not have experienced directly, but would be able to apply other things you are familiar with to identify them. Also, some people will have an easier time identifying the objects than other people. We each experience things differently and understand things our own way.

Our faith can work similar to reaching into that bag to identify the objects. What we currently feel spiritually combines in our hearts and minds with the things we have experienced in the past to lead us to believe in those things that we do not see now, but that we hope exist. Just as with that bag of objects, sometimes our experience with faith will be harder than other times, especially as we encounter something not completely familiar. Just as with that bag of objects, sometimes it will seem that someone has an easy time with faith while we may feel we have a harder time with it. If the bag contained an unfamiliar object, it could be hard to identify. Spiritually speaking, we may come across situations that feel unfamiliar to us, and it can be more difficult to exercise faith. In our spiritual lives of faith, it may be that the only experience we've had with something is the hope we have for it—the longing after it and seeing it in our mind. We may be unable to identify a completely unfamiliar object from the bag, but in our spiritual lives, through faith, we can recognize the feeling in our heart associated with feeling after the things we have hoped for, even as we experience them for the first time.

With that bag of objects, we literally gain comprehension of the object through the experience of feeling it. I believe faith is the same way: we gain spiritual comprehension by experience and by feeling it. The Definition of Faith is about understanding faith spiritually. The examples of faith in action from the sections The Vision of Faith and The Focus of Faith really are necessary to provide context for our understanding of faith. Faith is a principle of action, and I can think of no better way to understand it than to see how to apply it and make it active in our lives. That is how we will gain an understanding of how faith becomes a part of us.

As we introduce the Definition of Faith, those familiar with doctrines of the Church of Jesus Christ of Latter-day

Saints may be familiar with Alma 32:21, and immediately say that is one place where the Definition of Faith is found. That verse is often quoted in LDS discussions of faith. Turning to that verse, we read that Alma teaches: "Faith is not to have a perfect knowledge of things; therefore if ye have faith ye hope for things which are not seen, which are true."

I have to admit that at first I had a hard time understanding this verse as a clear definition of what faith really is. I don't mean to be too literal here, but Alma starts by saying "faith is not," and I wanted to know what faith *is*. He then says that "if ye have faith, ye hope for things," and again, this isn't exactly what faith *is*, but what someone with faith *does*. To me, those statements didn't really explain what I wanted to know for years, which was the answer of what faith really is. Alma also says that if you have faith you "hope for things which are not seen, which are true." But does that mean hope and faith are the same thing? Does something being true or not true really make the difference between faith and *not* faith, when what I want in the first place is to know what is true?

Maybe I thought too deeply about something simple. But you can see that I had a lot of questions. Maybe you have also had a lot of similar questions. I felt like faith was something just outside the reach of my understanding, and so I couldn't really exercise great faith, because I couldn't understand *how* to exercise great faith. We talked about examples of great faith, but what enabled the people in those examples to exercise such great faith?

Well, if I couldn't get a complete Definition of Faith from Alma 32:21, I know that Paul also talks about faith in Hebrews 11, which is also often quoted in discussions of faith. Paul says: "Now, faith is the substance of things hoped for, the evidence of things not seen" (Hebrews 11:1). This strikes me as pretty interesting because Paul at least starts off by saying "faith is."

Still, what does the "substance of things hoped for" mean? Is that substance the same or different from the "evidence of things not seen"? If we believe the same God inspired both verses of scripture, what does Hebrews 11:1 have to do with Alma 32:21?

The footnote in the LDS King James Version of the Bible can help us on this one, as we learn that the word translated here as *substance* can alternately be translated as "assurance, basis, or foundation" (Hebrews 11:1, footnote *b*). As I read it, faith is the basis or foundation of our hope. It is the assurance we feel that the thing we hope for will become reality. And that assurance needs to be felt to have an impact on us—it needs to be experienced!

Both Alma and Paul mention hope. Maybe we're starting to understand faith a little as we understand that we must have hope in something to be able to have faith in it. Faith keeps us moving toward the realization of that hope or toward that hope becoming reality, because we are assured that it will happen. We hope the Lord is faithful and carries through on His promises, and we feel assurance that He is faithful from prior experience or from the assurance of the Holy Spirit to keep us moving toward the expected outcome. The Apostle Paul further says that faith is "the evidence of things not seen." We do not yet see it or have it, which is why we hope for it—it is something we anticipate.

But this isn't just something we look forward to without a reason to think it will happen. We probably all know we can create hope out of nothing, or believe in fairy tales. I can find belief, even if illogical or unfounded. I can even choose to deny a reality that I see right in front of me to hope for something that I would like to be true. However, Paul doesn't just say to hope in some abstract way—he brings in the concept of "evidence." There should be an assurance to accompany our hope.

Instead of creating hope from nothing or choosing to believe in something where there is no basis, I can rely on "proof" or evidence. But again, what is that evidence and where does it come from? Is that the same as scientific or legal evidence? What assurances are there?

A Two-Way Street of Trust

Imagine I place in front of you two clear containers, one with a clear liquid, and the other with a white powdery substance. Now imagine I told you to combine some of the liquid with some of the powder. As you pour in the liquid, the combination begins to fizz and bubble, until the combined bubbly substance fills up the container and flows over the top.

Just based on this description, would you know what the white powder and the clear liquid are? Maybe you could correctly guess that the liquid is white vinegar and the white powder is baking soda. The reaction is caused by the combination of the acid component of the vinegar (acetic acid) with the baking soda, which is a base. Acids and bases generally neutralize each other and result in a solution of water and some leftover minerals, which are scientifically considered a salt (which can include more than just the salt on your dinner table). What is really cool, however, about baking soda and vinegar is that before forming salt and water, they first form another compound (carbonic acid), which is unstable and immediately breaks down into carbon dioxide and water. The carbon dioxide is what makes the foaming bubbles.

If you knew what the white powder and the clear liquid were, I am guessing it is because you have either seen this experiment before or maybe done it yourself. Maybe you have just heard someone say it works, and since it is someone you trust, you were confident you knew the answer. In any case, the reason you would *expect* this reaction is because of your previous experience with the same reaction, which reminds us of the bag of objects we reach into. Your previous experience could be firsthand if you witnessed the experiment yourself, or secondhand if you heard about it from someone you trust. Either way your experience leads you to expect what will happen.

Now imagine if I told you that you could get the same effect by combining vinegar and salt. Would you believe me? Maybe you would be skeptical because you have never heard of anyone combining vinegar and salt to get that reaction. Maybe you would be skeptical if you knew about the science of acids and bases, and you knew that combining an acid with salt cannot make the same thing happen. The bottom line is that you could be skeptical both because of your lack of experience with the proposed experiment or because some knowledge makes you believe you understand how things actually work.

Of course, if you have never seen baking soda combined with vinegar you could always just try putting them together to see if you get the same reaction you have heard of. If I tell you that vinegar combines with salt in the same way and you are not sure, you could also just experiment with combining the salt and vinegar to see what happens. The key is letting your initial skepticism turn into curiosity until you are willing to try the experiment. But you will have to follow the experiment to get "proof" or evidence. You cannot expect the same evidence by just trying your own thing, even if you think your own thing is similar. As you gain experience, you will start to form an expectation. That experience will better enable you to seek after the objective of your experiment. You spiritually test out the word of God through the exercise of faith by experimenting on God's word. As you do that, you will be in a situation where you can spiritually "reach into a bag of objects" and recognize faith by a combination of feeling it and comparing it to your previous experience.

We talked about a science experiment to introduce evidence or proof and to introduce an experiment with faith as set out in scripture. Our question when reading Hebrews 11 was "What is the evidence Paul talks about, and where does it come from?" Another question we had was "How does Paul's discussion of faith relate to Alma's discussion of faith?" We're going to address those questions in light of the science experiment we just talked about. The answers build on things we have already discussed.

Let's look at Hebrews 11 again: "Now, faith is the substance of things hoped for, the evidence of things not seen. For by it the elders obtained a good report" (Hebrews 11:1–2). Notice that I added verse 2 this time, which informs us that "elders obtained a good report." The footnote tells us that "obtained a good report" can mean "received witness, testimony" (Hebrews 11:2, footnote *a*). But, to be quite honest with you, that verse had never seemed interesting to me until I read it in Portuguese. In the João Ferreira de Almeida Portuguese Bible, Hebrews 11:1–2 reads as: "*Ora, a fé é o firme fundamento das coisas que se esperam, e a prova das coisas que se não vêem. Porque por ela os antigos alcançaram testemunho.*" I am not a Portuguese scholar, but I will attempt to make a literal translation of this into English: "Behold, faith is the firm foundation [or basis, or assurance] of things that are hoped for, and the proof [or evidence] of things that are not seen. Because by it [faith], those of former times obtained witness [or testimony]."

There are a few things that I want to highlight from these verses. The first is that the translation in Portuguese reads consistent with the alternate Hebrew translation provided in the LDS King James Version footnotes. The next thing is that the expression in Portuguese (*a prova*) that is translated as "the evidence" in the King James Version comes from the verb *provar*, meaning "to prove," as through a trial or test. Basically, my understanding is that there is an implication that the foundation or evidence of things hoped for comes from putting the things to the test. That's just like the action we mentioned above. That reminds me of the experience we've talked about that we get as we reach into the bag of objects or do the experiment with vinegar. Another interesting thing is that the word for "obtaining" or "receiving" testimony is the verb *alcançar*, which I understand to mean putting out some effort to get something—you reach something after reaching for it, rather than having it come find you.

Lastly, my translation of verse 2 starts off with the word *because*, which could also be translated into English as "for" in the sense of meaning that one thing leads to another. The word *because* in English includes the word *cause* right in it. The word in the Portuguese version that I translate as "because" is a combination of two words that mean "through which" or "by which." Essentially, we see that faith is the thing through which those we read about in scripture went out and obtained their witnesses based on what they experienced. Those witnesses are many: the reality of and the faithfulness of God, His mercy and goodness, His justice and judgment. They received witness of the power that God has, and witness that His children can see the exercise of that power through their own faith.

This look into the Portuguese intrigued me enough that I decided to do a little academic research. I found that the Greek and Latin words from which our English word *faith* is derived have to do with "trust" and "trustworthiness."[2] That leads to an interesting observation: the root words from which the expressions *faith*, *faithfulness*, and *trustworthiness* are derived mean basically the same thing and center on the concept of trust. A key understanding of faith as used throughout scripture is that people *trusted* in God, and they trusted to the extent that they did what the Lord asked under any circumstance. They were motivated to such obedience because they trusted that the Lord blesses those who obey Him. They trusted that God always leads us in the best path, no matter how the path appears to our carnal, fallen minds. They trusted in how God deals with His children. Ultimately, we learn to trust God because He is faithful. We have the evidence of His trustworthiness. We have our own testimony of being blessed when we obey and the testimonies of those who have put God's trustworthiness to the test, all of which give us assurance. We have the evidence of the accounts in scripture. Faith is about putting our trust in God and being committed to carrying through on our end, just as those who "obtained a good report" did.

I feel like I understand the concept of God's faithfulness. He is trustworthy, so we can trust Him. And interestingly, we show that we trust by being faithful ourselves—by acting in ways consistent with our trust, and being faithful to God's word. I like to say that the path of faith is a two-way street of trust. It is not one sided or one-dimensional, and is not based on wishful thinking on our part, but is a two-way relationship with God based on His words. We learn that we can always trust God to do what He says, and because we can, we act faithfully in accordance with God's faithfulness. As our faith grows, we show that we are trustworthy by following God's word in faith, which we do because God is trustworthy to come through on His word.

Wait a second! Now I want to go back and read Alma's words again. He says in Alma 32:21, "And now as I said concerning faith—faith is not to have a perfect knowledge of things; therefore if ye have faith ye hope for things which are not seen, which are true." Maybe I can start to see why Alma may have been interested in telling us what faith is not and what someone with faith does. I think Alma's main point is that faith is not about absolute certainty. Consider the lead-up to verse 21 from these verses: "Yea, there are many who do say: If thou wilt show unto us a sign from heaven, then we shall know of a surety; then we shall believe. Now I ask, is this faith? Behold, I say unto you, Nay; for if a man knoweth a thing he hath no cause to believe, for he knoweth it" (Alma 32:17–18). If with faith we do not have absolute certainty, I think the significant point is that we cannot wait for certainty before we are willing to act in faith. Said another way, we will have to act before we obtain certainty. We'll have to experiment before we know for sure which things are true. Those will be acts of trust, based on assurance that things are true—that will be our faith.

Think about someone you trust. The more you know that person, the more you trust them. You may know them so well that you feel certain you know what they will do in certain circumstances. The reality is that you do not have absolute certainty about what the person will do. You cannot really ever have absolute certainty about what the person will do, because they have their agency to act however they want. The primary difference with God is that He does exactly what He says He will—always. We can have certainty, absolute certainty, that God is faithful. The challenge with that is we do not always understand His ways in doing what He says, even though He is always faithful (see Isaiah 55:8–9).

Your trust that a person will come through for you increases more each time you experience their trustworthiness. Your trust in God will grow in a similar way. Your trust to allow God to come through however He thinks best will also increase as you come to see that He is always faithful and wise. The trick, of course, is to understand what God says He will do. Faith is about what we do and how we live as a result of knowing that God will do what He says He will do. When we act in faith, we actually start moving toward the thing we anticipate happening because we believe God will bring it about and bless us for moving in that direction.

OK, so we were looking at Paul's words in Hebrews 11:1–2 and wondering where evidence comes from. We were also wondering what those verses had to do with Alma's explanation of aspects of faith in Alma 32:21. Now we've seen that faith is primarily related to trust, and the more experience we get with God, the more our trust increases. We also talked about a science experiment where we combine baking soda and vinegar. Regarding that experiment, remember the following as we go into the next part of our discussion: you expect the reaction because of your previous experience with it; you may initially be skeptical where you have no experience; and you can always try the experiment to see if you get the result you expect. You must allow curiosity and a sincere desire to learn to overcome skepticism for long enough to try the experiment.

Alma describes an experiment upon the word of God, and in essence putting the word to the test to obtain evidence. I like to think that Alma's experiment will tell us how to get the evidence or assurance Paul talks about. Alma says: "Now, as I said concerning faith—that it was not a perfect knowledge—even so it is with my words. Ye cannot know of their surety at first, unto perfection, any more than faith is a perfect knowledge" (Alma 32:26). Alma tells us that he is going to further explain what he started talking about in verse 21 by reminding us that faith is not a perfect knowledge. So if faith is not a perfect knowledge, what is it? He still doesn't tell us directly in the next verses, at least not in terms of coming out and saying, "Here's what faith is." However, what he does is walk through the steps of building faith: "But behold, if ye will awake and arouse your faculties, even to *an experiment upon my words*, and exercise a particle of faith, yea, even if ye can no more than *desire to believe*, let this desire work in you, even until ye believe in a manner that ye can give place for a portion of my words" (Alma 32:27; emphasis added).

First, we must awaken something inside us that causes us to desire to understand. I referred to curiosity with the science experiment earlier—we want to know. In the context of faith, that curiosity will include a yearning for light. And it must be strong enough to perform a spiritual experiment instead of just academically evaluating something. A spiritual experiment requires us to change what we think about, and change our behaviors. A spiritual experiment takes place inside us, instead of simply observing what's around us. Ultimately Alma teaches us we should cultivate a desire from belief into faith and finally into perfect knowledge. Notice that he starts out telling us to experiment, and to desire to believe. Actually, he starts by telling us what faith is not, and then telling us to experiment on what faith is.

Next, we must hold onto our trust as we work on what is inside of us. Perhaps some of us are simply not in a place where it is easy to start experimenting and exercising faith. Some of us have a genuinely hard time trusting. But even those who are at the lowest starting point of faith can use the same process of experimentation and learning to exercise faith. We first desire something, feeling a need for something more within us. Those who feel no need have a remarkable reluctance to experimenting on something unfamiliar. We allow that desire to work within us until we are ready to take a chance on it.

Isn't this the same as any new trust relationship? First, we have to be willing to interact with someone new. We must give at least a small amount of trust to see if someone is trustworthy. Sometimes we are so guarded in our trust that we have to start out by just giving the person a chance. Maybe your faith is like that right now. But give the Lord a chance to prove He is faithful. We give the Lord a chance to prove He is faithful by giving our trust in obedience to His word. Our obedience is the experiment. We do not give the Lord a chance to prove He is faithful by requiring Him to give us a sign. This is very important to understand: the Lord has already set out the general terms of the relationship at least as far as our behavior is concerned. He does this because He really does know better. The relationship requires our obedience to experiment to see if He is faithful in blessing us for keeping His commandments. That is how we "give the Lord a chance," so to speak. We do not set the terms of the relationship by telling the Lord that we will believe if He does something we want. Such requests on our part are not based on faith but selfishness and pride. With selfishness, we issue a challenge to the Lord, while at the same time showing that we are not willing to experiment on the Lord. Instead, I encourage you to experiment on His words by obeying them.

Now we need to remember that just because we tried the experiment once, we are not done gaining and exercising faith. I think the key to what Alma tells us is that the *process* for gaining and for exercising faith is always the same—whether we have a little or a lot of it. Until we have a perfect knowledge of the specific thing or circumstance we are encountering, we must go through the process associated with learning and gaining faith each time. Every experience and every circumstance will likely feel similar at the start of the faith process. It's sort of like reaching into that bag of objects and trying to identify something we've only heard about but haven't actually held before. It's like putting baking soda and vinegar together because we're told to do it and seeing something cool happen. And we will gain perfect knowledge through the same faith process, no matter what the circumstance is, whether familiar or unfamiliar.

Let's reflect for a moment. I started out by saying that Alma tells us what faith is not, and tells us what someone with faith will do. Paul tells us what faith is, which is based on trust in God. We trust based on evidence or assurance by putting the word of God to the test. Alma provides us with a process to understand how to gain and exercise faith, which is based on experimenting with the word of God (or putting it to the test) to gain evidence of it. Wow! Ultimately, what I had been looking for over the years is explained a lot better than I realized, and right where everyone told me to look for it. I had simply failed to understand it. I think my main setback in understanding was in thinking that I could test the Lord under my own conditions, when really we are invited to come and test out *His conditions* to prove Him faithful. He has provided the word, which we are invited to use to prove His faithfulness. We will feel His will and know the things we should do by which we will prove the Lord's faithfulness to His promises, rather than challenging Him to bend to our will. We learn to trust, even as we work on becoming trustworthy.

Faith Comes by the Word of God

The more I learn, the more I recognize that Alma's analogy to a seed is very powerful. The first step to seeing if a seed is good is by *doing something with it*. That is the experiment.

The seed is the word, and the first thing we do to experiment with the word to see if it is trustworthy is to do something with it—we must adapt our behavior to it. We plant the seed in our hearts by hearing and obeying the word, and the seed will then sprout. The key to building our faith is likewise *doing something with it.* I cannot emphasize enough that the way to faith is not to set up conditions that we require the Lord to meet before we agree to have faith. He has already set up numerous conditions for receiving blessings. Prove His faithfulness by trying one of the conditions you have a hard time with. That will plant the seed of faith in rich soil. As you see it grow, your faith will be started. Then follow along with the rest of Alma's explanation of what to do with that seedling to turn it into the tree of testimony.

Alma puts it this way: "Now, we will compare the word unto a seed. Now, if ye give place, that a seed may be planted in your heart, behold, if it be a true seed, or a good seed, if ye do not cast it out by your unbelief, that ye will resist the Spirit of the Lord, behold, it will begin to swell within your breasts; and when you feel these swelling motions, ye will begin to say within yourselves—It must needs be that this is a good seed, or that the word is good, for it beginneth to enlarge my soul; yea, it beginneth to enlighten my understanding, yea, it beginneth to be delicious to me. Now behold, would not this increase your faith? I say unto you, Yea; nevertheless it hath not grown up to a perfect knowledge. But behold, as the seed swelleth, and sprouteth, and beginneth to grow, then you must needs say that the seed is good; for behold it swelleth, and sprouteth, and beginneth to grow. And now, behold, will not this strengthen your faith? Yea, it will strengthen your faith: for ye will say I know that this is a good seed; for behold it sprouteth and beginneth to grow. And now, behold, are ye sure that this is a good seed? I say unto you, Yea; for every seed bringeth forth unto its own likeness" (Alma 32:28–31).

You will know the seed is good when you feel peace confirm your choice of actions or when you feel in your heart that your choice to experiment upon the word has brought the blessing promised for that obedience. Your seedling of faith will then grow as you see the blessings come into your life, and you will begin to recognize that the Lord really does know best. Remember, you are experimenting on or testing the word here. You will know if the word is from God as follows: "Therefore, if a seed groweth it is good, but if it groweth not, behold it is not good, therefore it is cast away. And now, behold, because ye have tried the experiment, and planted the seed, and it swelleth and sprouteth, and beginneth to grow, ye must needs know that the seed is good" (Alma 32:32–33).

Now remember what I am proposing here: one of Alma's points in writing was to help us understand how we go from little or no faith in something to a perfect knowledge. We get there by experimenting, as we discussed experimenting with baking soda and vinegar. Alma wants us to understand that we have to act before we will know. We do this in steps. We first gain a perfect knowledge that the seed is good, because we planted it, watered it, and it grew. Alma continues: "And now, behold, is your knowledge perfect? Yea, your knowledge is perfect in that thing, and your faith is dormant; and this because you know, for ye know that the word hath swelled your souls, and ye also know that it hath sprouted up, that your understanding doth begin to be enlightened, and your mind doth begin to expand" (Alma 32:34). When we talk about starting out not knowing, the first thing we will know is that the word is true and good. Since we know the seed is good, we now have a chance to develop that seed into a tree of testimony that brings fruit into our lives.

Verse 35 talks about feeling or recognizing the truth because it is light. Verse 36 indicates that we know the seed was good because we tried the experiment. Then we read: "And behold, as the tree beginneth to grow, ye will say: Let us nourish it with great care, that it may get root, that it may grow up, and bring forth fruit unto us. And now behold, if ye nourish it with much care it will get root, and grow up, and bring forth fruit. . . . But if ye will nourish the word, yea, nourish the tree as it beginneth to grow, by your faith with great diligence, and with patience, looking forward to the fruit thereof, it shall take root; and behold it shall be a tree springing up unto everlasting life" (Alma 32:37, 41).

Let's see what we know up to this point about the process of exercising faith: first, we desire enough to experiment upon the word—we build up some hope that the thing can be true; second, we put the word to the test by obeying it—we recognize its goodness by the assurances it brings even as it provides evidence of God's faithfulness; third, we nourish it by continuing in obedience and diligence; and fourth, we have an expectation of the fruit because the tree is growing and doing well. This can happen anew in each circumstance where we need to apply faith. This process should be repeated over and over again throughout our lives as each new circumstance and challenge in life brings uncertainty that needs to be addressed through faith.

Now, speaking of the fruit, I want to ask this: How long does it take for a tree to start producing fruit? What is the fruit in Alma's analogy, anyway? And how long does it take for the tree Alma talks about to reach its full size and maturity? I don't think there are clear-cut answers to these questions. Different amounts of time are required for different kinds of trees, and the same will be true for different people in different circumstances. But there are a couple of things I think are likely to be common for all of us: The first is that it can takes years for most any kind of tree to start producing fruit after the seed is planted. So, we may have a tree for years before we can enjoy the fruit from it. I don't think faith takes years to start producing the fruit of testimony, but it may take time. And the longer we are willing to nourish the tree, the more fruit we will gain. The second thing is that trees don't stop growing. They are not like animals that reach maturity and then stop—trees always grow for as long as they are alive. And so we should expect it to be with our testimony: it will take time for us to nurture our faith from a seedling into a mature tree of testimony, and we must never stop nourishing it, as it will grow all our lives.

So what is that fruit? I think it will be something different for each individual in different circumstances, but whatever it is will be food and enjoyment to our soul—something that will nourish us and that can also be shared to nourish someone else. Additionally, fruit houses new seeds. Each tree of testimony we grow will mature into a source of perfect knowledge and blessing. Maybe it will take longer than we want to get it there. Fruit probably will not come immediately, but once our faith (and our trust in the Lord's faithfulness) begins to turn into a testimony (a sure expectation of how God will act), it will never stop growing as long as we keep it alive. Even a mature tree requires nourishing and patience to obtain the fruit. And unfortunately, even a mature tree can die through neglect and drought. Sometimes, our faith will be like certain citrus trees I have seen that seem to produce fruit year-round. Other times in life, our faith will be like a traditional fruit tree, where there are seasons of patient waiting followed by seasons of fruitful abundance.

Hopefully all of this gives us a better understanding of the Definition of Faith. For me, it also leads to another question:

How do you know when you have faith? The answer I would give is that action is the companion of trust and expectation. So when you act, you have faith in something. Planting the seed is action. Action and the ability to act are where power comes from. Faith, ultimately, carries power. The power of faith is the power of connection between us and the thing in which we have faith. Hopefully, we base our most important faith in God. When we have faith in God and His power, we act in ways consistent with that faith. It is shown most evidently by our willingness to obey God's word. Significantly, faith brings light, strength, and power into our lives when we act on it.

Now with a better understanding of the Definition of Faith, we can see deeper meaning in verses that expound on faith. I want to look at a couple more verses from Hebrews to show this. In Hebrews 12:1–2, we read: "Wherefore seeing we also are compassed about with so great a cloud of witnesses, let us lay aside every weight, and the sin which doth so easily beset us, and let us run with patience the race that is set before us, Looking unto Jesus the author and finisher of our faith; who for the joy that was set before him endured the cross, despising the shame, and is set down at the right hand of the throne of God."

Paul says that Jesus is the "author and finisher of our faith," which he says should be apparent because of all the witnesses we have, and which should cause us to lay aside our sin and do whatever God asks of us (or run whatever race is set before us). Jesus is the *author* of our faith because He is trustworthy, which enables us to trust Him. He always comes through with His promises. His trustworthiness inspires our confidence to try His word and leads us along as we experience the fulfillment of His promised blessings. Thus, He is the author because we can begin exercising faith because of

His faithfulness. He is the *finisher* of our faith because in the end it is He who will reward every action we make based on that trust. That is why we should lay aside all our sins, trusting that Jesus took those sins upon Himself. That is why we can lay aside every weight and run the race set before us, trusting that He descended below everything and grants us the gift to live free from our burdens and look forward to a better life. We run whatever race is set before us because we trust that the Lord leads us along the path, or the Journey of Faith. No matter what race that is, and no matter what path that is, we will have God's help as we act in faith or take the journey, trusting ourselves to the Lord. The path we take in faith provides us a chance to work with God as we cultivate the relationship that comes with a two-way street of trust.

This leads in well to another verse on faith. Recall one of my original questions about Alma 32:21: I was concerned that verse doesn't say directly what faith is. We looked and found out what Paul says in Hebrews, and then we came back and perhaps saw a reason why Alma doesn't say directly what faith is. Both Paul and Alma talked about faith in terms of hope. So, I suppose this discussion wouldn't be complete unless we also discussed the following. Ether 12:6 states: "And now, I, Moroni, would speak somewhat concerning these things; I would show unto the world that faith is things which are hoped for and not seen; wherefore, dispute not because ye see not, for ye receive no witness until after the trial of your faith."

I can see that it sure sounds like Moroni says what faith is ("faith is things which are hoped for"). Still, I think this verse is consistent with everything we learned from Paul and Alma. Let's put this verse into context. In Ether 12, we are introduced to the prophet Ether, who goes out to preach to a society that had lost its way. Ether taught "that by faith all things are fulfilled" at the end of verse 3. In verse 4, Ether continues: "Wherefore, whoso believeth in God might with surety hope for a better world, yea, even a place at the right hand of God, which hope cometh of faith, maketh an anchor to the souls of men, which would make them sure and steadfast, always abounding in good works, being led to glorify God." In verse 5, we read that Ether preached many things to this society or people, "which they did not believe, because they saw them not." And then comes verse 6, which is already quoted above.

Now let's recall that we're going to think of faith as a two-way street of trust. The word *faith* is derived from a root word referring to "trusting" and "trustworthiness." In English, we have no pure verb form of *faith*. In scripture, we frequently see the words *believe* and *trust* used to call to mind the concept of faith. The faith we're talking about isn't just "trust" in someone or something, where we put our trust on the line and hope God comes through. It is possible for trust to only go one direction, but faith goes both directions. Thus, we cannot think of the faith words in scripture as some vague trust feeling. Rather, the belief and trust of true faith is a focused feeling in our heart and soul that brings out action on our part.

Starting back in Ether at verse 3, we read that all things are fulfilled by faith, and we can understand that every promise God ever makes will be fulfilled. He is faithful, and because He is, everything He says will be fulfilled. Verse 4 begins by saying "wherefore," which brings to mind a cause-and-effect relationship. Now, I call it a cause-and-effect relationship as a shorthand, but what I really mean is that it ties two related things together. The gist is that in scripture you will read a cause or a condition or some other form of lead-up statement, and then the word *wherefore*, and then the effect or explanation or command or counsel or some other thing directly related to that lead-up statement. We could almost read *wherefore* as "and so it follows." So generally when you see *wherefore* in the scriptures, you are about to read the effect or the thing that follows, and the cause or lead-in will have been introduced previously. When *wherefore* starts a verse, the cause was introduced in a preceding verse or verses. "Wherefore," when we put our trust in God, by living our lives in a way that shows we believe what He has said, we have assurance of a better world. We live in hope because of our trust that God is faithful, which anchors our souls to make us so firm in our conviction that we will always do what God asks us to do.

The people to whom Ether preached had lost such faith. As we read their full story in the Book of Ether, we learn that they put their trust in themselves, in wicked men, and in the riches of the earth. And as happens to all who put their whole heart and whole trust into something or someone that cannot deliver on its words, their heart is broken and their trust dashed to pieces when the object of their trust is exposed as being untrustworthy or unable to deliver on the hoped-for outcome. That is not true faith, but illusion. And sometimes we might claim God is the object of trust in which we lose our faith. There are a lot of reasons we might make that claim, and many of them make sense to me. But my experience has always been that even as we claim God has broken our trust, it is not because He is unfaithful. Rather, we have made a requirement that we will only trust in Him if He fulfills *our* wishes, instead of our turning our hearts to God's will.

And so it is that the people didn't believe Ether—they trusted in things that could not deliver an outcome, or they trusted in an outcome that could not be delivered, and so they had spent their trust unwisely only to see it dashed to pieces. Then we hear Moroni's counsel: faith is that hope we just talked about in verse 4, and we don't have to see an immediate result to make our conviction to live right (the cause); "wherefore," don't discount God's promises because you haven't seen them fulfilled yet, because you have not put faith to the test when you act as they did (the effect). We could also rephrase this as: faith is based on what we don't already have (the condition), "wherefore," accept the trial of faith so that you can receive the thing you hope for (the command). Again, as we saw with Alma, we have to act before we know. As we saw with Paul, we receive assurance of things we do not yet see.

The Definition of Faith is supposed to help us understand what faith is and how to apply it in our lives. I believe that the better we can apply faith in our lives, and the stronger the faith we can apply, the better our lives will be. We may be starting with weak faith and want to someday have great faith. We may already have some experience with faith and want to know how to improve it. In the following two accounts we see a circumstance where Jesus chastises a man for his lack of faith, and then we see a circumstance in which Jesus praises a man for the depth of his faith. The difference in the stories is where they were with respect to the word of God. This is that seed Alma talked about. Watch what each person does with the word presented to them. Then ask yourself where you are currently at with your faith, and use the principles we've discussed to increase your faith. I think most of us will fall somewhere in between these two stories, but the principles work no matter where you are currently at. As Alma teaches us, whether our faith is weak or strong, we follow the same process to increase it.

In Mark 9, we read of a man who came before Jesus for help with a problem with his son: "And when [Jesus] came to his disciples [from the Mount of Transfiguration], he saw a great multitude about them, and the scribes questioning with them. . . . And he asked the scribes, What question ye with them? And one of the multitude answered and said, Master, I have brought unto thee my son, which hath a dumb spirit; And wheresoever he taketh him, he teareth him: and he foameth, and gnasheth with his teeth, and pineth away: and I spake to thy disciples that they should cast him out; and they could not. He answereth him, and saith, O faithless generation, how long shall I be with you? how long shall I suffer you? bring him unto me" (Mark 9:14–19).

We could spend a long time discussing whether this final statement of rebuke was meant specifically for the father, or for the disciples, or maybe for the scribes, or others listening in on the exchange. However, remembering that the scripture stories are *our* stories, we can learn something by thinking of reasons the rebuke might be for any of them. The point is that Jesus issues a rebuke, which we can think of as a teaching opportunity to point out something that someone needs to work on. In each case here, for the scribes, the disciples, the father, and the crowd, they can use some strengthening of their faith in receiving the word of God. By extension, this rebuke can be to each of us in our varying circumstances when we struggle with our faith.

To really understand how our story applies to how we receive the word of God, we need to set up a little more context. Let's go back to Mark 6:7–13, where Jesus gave His disciples power to heal and sent them out into the world to perform His work and spread His doctrine. They were told to minister the word Jesus had given them. When we consider Matthew 15:26, Matthew 28:16–20, and Acts 1:8, we can understand that this empowerment of the disciples was part of a bigger work Jesus was establishing. As important and powerful as His personal ministry was, Jesus was establishing something larger than personal ministry to the precious few He could reach in His short earthly ministry.

Knowing that these disciples had been empowered with the word to do the works Jesus had been doing, perhaps we can better understand how the rebuke could be directed to the scribes who were skeptical of the disciples and Jesus, who questioned their words as well as their power and authority to act. Perhaps we can better understand how the rebuke could be directed to the disciples who could not seem to exercise the power they had been given through the word of Jesus Himself. Perhaps we can better understand how the rebuke could be directed to this poor father who had asked the disciples for help but appears to have lacked faith in their words of blessing, or the power given to them. Regardless of which disbelief I look at, I'm pretty sure I've personally experienced it. Maybe that is true for you too. So, this rebuke can be an invitation for you.

Let's look a little closer at Jesus's rebuke. Notice that the rebuke is actually two back-to-back questions. I have noticed that back-to-back in scripture can be a guide for self-examination or introspection. When there is a series of uninterrupted questions, the questions tend to have a main point, and build on each other, which guides our introspection. In this case, after calling out the "faithless generation," Jesus asks: "How long shall I be with you?" and "How long shall I suffer you?" I see these specific questions as relating to the main theme of the "faithless generation."

Just as we saw above that the rebuke could apply to at least three different types of a lack of faith or lack of receiving the word, this rebuke can likewise provide some insight into each type of lack of faith. When I think of not receiving the word as the scribes did not, the questions "How long shall I be with you?" and "How long shall I suffer you?" remind me that I might not keep getting opportunities to receive the word if I continue to harden my heart and reject it. I have to make my heart open and lay aside my skepticism so that I might experiment on the word and choose faith. How long will the Lord suffer my rejection of the word before He allows me to receive justice instead of mercy?

When I think of not exercising faith in the words that empower me and allow me to act in the duties of faith to bless and serve others, like the disciples, the questions "How long shall I be with you?" and "How long shall I suffer you?" remind me that the Lord expects me to act in faith now with what I have been blessed with. The Lord expects me to become something through faith and to act in faith with the talents and capacities He has blessed me with. Reliance on the Lord in faith does not mean I wait to act until I receive specific instructions. Rather, I allow the word to empower me to act with the capacities and talents the Lord has blessed me with (see Doctrine and Covenants 58:26–29), trusting He will magnify my talent as I magnify my calling to serve. How long will the Lord suffer my failure to act on my own righteous initiative before I lose the reward of acting in faith?

When I think of not having the faith to believe that the word can help me, as the father, the questions "How long shall I be with you?" and "How long shall I suffer you?" remind me that the Lord extends mercy to me at every opportunity, if I will but turn to God and receive it (see, for example, Romans 10:21, Mosiah 6:12, and 3 Nephi 9:14). Similar to opening my heart to receive faith, I can exercise faith on the word of the Lord to turn to God and receive His mercy and blessings. How long will I keep the Lord waiting and suffering with me in my heartache before I am willing to let go of fears and doubts to receive the word to allow the Lord to bless me?

We focused on the rebuke here for a bit, but after the rebuke, our story continues: "And they brought him unto him: and when he saw him, straightway the spirit tare him; and he fell on the ground, and wallowed foaming. And he asked his father, How long is it ago since this came unto him? And he said, Of a child. And ofttimes it hath cast him into the fire, and into the waters, to destroy him: but if thou canst do any thing, have compassion on us, and help us" (Mark 9:20–22). With the father's last statement, we learn a little more about the situation. This man must have struggled with this issue for years, and felt the pain of a helpless parent watching his child suffer.

He appears to be almost to the point of not having any faith left, as he has now come to the Savior Himself, and says to Him: "if thou canst do any thing. . . ." To me, the father is starting to doubt why he came to Jesus at all. It seems to me that this man may not have been ready at the hands of the disciples to receive a blessing, especially in light of the lack of faith of the scribes who were around. He was deeply troubled and deeply hurt, with a son who was sorely afflicted. Jesus later teaches His disciples that some exercises of faith like this require something more to apply (see Mark 9:28–29), so there is also the possibility that the disciples provided a somewhat timid exercise of faith in trying to help him.

This father's faith is at such a weakened state that, even at the feet of the Savior, he is unsure that Jesus could or would do anything. Surely this man has suffered a crisis of faith, or many of them. I think we have a man who wants to believe but has forgotten how. I've been in similar places and feel compassion for any who experience it. Such feelings can make it very difficult to accept the word of God, and thus, to generate faith.

Now recall the words of James that we looked at previously that said we are to believe, not wavering, and not being double-minded (James 1:6–8). It appears to me that this father doubted heavily, filled with fear, and thus was double-minded. He brought his child to Jesus to be healed, but once there he was unsure that Jesus could or would do anything for them. Jesus's response to the man is gentle and guiding, and yet demanding: "If thou canst believe, all things are possible to him that believeth" (Mark 9:23). Notice that Jesus's response made clear that the issue was not whether Jesus (or His disciples) had power but whether the man would trust in it. Would he trust in the word? Would he trust in the work Jesus was setting up? Jesus didn't say, "Of course I can, let me take care of your son." That would have taken care of the needs of the son, but Jesus instead made the experience much more powerful for the father by challenging him to join in the experience with faith.

Then we again see the father's struggle with double-mindedness as we read on: "And straightway the father of the child cried out, and said with tears, Lord, I believe; help thou mine unbelief" (Mark 9:24). I have often wondered what would cause this man to answer "straightway" that he believed, only to follow it up by pleading "help thou mine unbelief." I think this illustrates something that is likely to present itself in each of us when we face a crisis of faith. The fact is that we are scared, even though we may want to believe. We are double-minded because we fear, and letting go of that fear so that we can start to live in faith again (or for the first time) is very difficult. And wasn't that Jesus's invitation to the father, to let go of his fears and believe? Let that be an invitation to you personally. For our exercise of faith, ultimately the more important question is not about whether Jesus "[can] do any thing," but whether "[we can] believe" (Mark 9:22–23). This will be directly related to our willingness and ability to receive and act on the word of God. That word motivates us to act in faith.

This account of the father can help us judge the depth of our faith. I like to ask myself these questions: Do I have a hard time believing what Jesus's appointed servants have said (do I believe the words of His servants)? Do I have to hear something over and over again before I am willing to believe it (do I accept the word)? Do I doubt the Lord's ability to carry out His word, or do I believe in His abilities for some people and some circumstances but feel that He won't do anything this time for me (do I really accept His words)? When I don't have a good answer to any of these questions, I usually have a fear that I just cannot seem to let go of, like the father in Mark 9. Think about what that fear might be for you so that at least you can address the real problem head-on. These questions might help: What doubts do I hold onto that prevent me from exercising faith? What underlying unbelief sabotages my profession of faith? What do I hold onto inside that prevents me from feeling and accepting God's word?

Let's contrast this father's story with the following story of a man who earned praise for his faith. In Matthew 8, we read: "And when Jesus was entered into Capernaum, there came unto him a centurion, beseeching him, And saying, Lord, my servant lieth at home sick of the palsy, grievously tormented. And Jesus saith unto him, I will come and heal him" (Matthew 8:5–7). Notice that Jesus offers to come and heal the servant of the centurion. However, "The centurion answered and said, Lord, I am not worthy that thou shouldest come under my roof: but speak the word only, and my servant shall be healed. . . . When Jesus heard it, he marvelled, and said to them that followed, Verily I say unto you, I have not found so great faith, no, not in Israel" (Matthew 8:8, 10).

The father in the previous story did not believe in the power of the disciples and doubted whether Jesus Himself could or would help. In contrast, the centurion trusted so much that all he required was for Jesus to "speak the word only" for his servant to be healed. The centurion goes on to explain in verse 9 that he understands how delegated authority works, which is directly in contrast to the father who did not believe in the power of the disciples. However, notice that the centurion apparently did not even require one of Jesus's disciples to come, but only that Jesus speak the word and His word would be carried out. In short, the centurion had faith enough to understand the power of the word. Perhaps that is why he earned the praise: "I have not found so great faith, no, not in Israel." The children of the kingdom had a hard time accepting the Savior, and many of them had an even harder time accepting the Savior's disciples. Despite the miracles, the people of Israel as a whole could not bring themselves to accept Jesus's words or the work He was trying to do. The centurion, however, had faith on Jesus and the power of His work and words. And we learn that "Jesus said unto the centurion, Go thy way; and as thou hast believed, so be it done unto thee. And his servant was healed in the selfsame hour" (Matthew 8:13).

There are two interesting points about these stories that I want to bring up. The first is the issue of self-worth. The second is regarding the "word of God." Regarding self-worth, in my experience, feeling that we are not worthy can be a barrier to faith. Especially in light of the stories about the father and the centurion—faith ultimately hinges on trust, and so even if we trust that the Lord can come through for us, if we believe that we are unworthy to receive help, we might think He won't help us. We may start to believe that He has all power to help, but that He will only help those we deem worthy of help. Notice that I said those *we* deem worthy of help. I specifically did not say those *He* deems worthy of help, because I believe there are some who would put far more restrictions on God's help than He would withhold His hand. Some do not have this concern of self-worth, but for others who do, it can be a challenge to exercising faith.

We could talk about the father, and perhaps he did not believe because he did not feel worthy of the help of the Savior. Our faith is often tried because we feel unworthy of the Savior. However, from the account of the centurion we learn that lacking self-worth does not mean you have to lack faith. He felt unworthy to the extent to deny Jesus's offer to come to his home, and yet trusted completely that the Savior could exercise power and would show compassion on the servant. Even if you don't feel worthy of God's help, allow Him to help. You can choose to be the centurion that believed in Jesus's power to help instead of the father, worrying that Jesus would not help. Typically, that feeling of unworthiness is a barrier we have put up because of our fear. Again, as discussed above, try to figure out exactly what that fear is, and ask the Lord for help to overcome it.

The second issue is about the "word of God." We can approach these two stories from the perspective of how these men trusted in the word of God. The father did not really believe the word, because he did not accept that Jesus's disciples were authorized or empowered to perform acts on His behalf. In contrast, the centurion believed so strongly in the word of God that he did not even need to see Jesus or His servants perform an act of healing, but merely have Jesus speak the word. This leads right into the words of Paul in Romans 10:17, "So then faith cometh by hearing, and hearing by the word of God." Based on this verse, though, I think the "hearing" he refers to is not just the something-I-heard-someone-say kind of hearing. This verse calls to my mind the words of Jesus when He said, "He that hath ears to hear, let him hear" (Matthew 11:15; see also Matthew 13:9, Mark 4:9, Mark 7:16, Luke 8:8, and Luke 14:35). Each time Jesus said this was when He had given a parable. The parables had different meanings for different people, depending on whether they applied their hearts, or the Heart of Faith, to understand the spiritual doctrine behind the words of the stories He told. And so I think Paul also tells us that faith comes to those that hear in the sense of applying their hearts to receive the words.

And what is that word? I want to look at this verse in two different ways. The first is simple and straightforward—the "word of God" is any word given by God Himself or one of His authorized servants. The Holy Spirit confirms the truth of these words. We hear such words and believe on them. Faith comes because we know that God is faithful and that when He speaks or inspires someone else to speak, whatever is said will come to pass. This is true whenever we hear the voice of the Spirit whispering words we can feel, or whether we receive confirmation of something said by another who speaks by that same Spirit. So, we trust what we hear, because what we hear is the word of God. Back now to the father and the centurion: one heard the words but struggled to apply his heart to believe the Savior would come through for him, while the other was so sure of the power of the Savior's words, he believed them even before they were spoken, for he knew they would be powerful.

The second way to look at Paul's words is that Jesus is the very embodiment of the word of God, in that He is the fulfillment of every promise ever made to the children of men. Jesus's perfect life was perfectly in line with the words God had given men to live by. John the Beloved said that "In the beginning was the Word, and the Word was with God, and the Word was God. . . . In him was life; and the life was the light of men. . . . And the Word was made flesh, and dwelt among us, (and we beheld his glory, the glory as of the only begotten of the Father,) full of grace and truth" (John 1:1, 4, 14). Jesus came to fulfill the promises made by God from the beginning. Jesus, full of grace and truth, is the Savior, the Mediator, to bring us back to dwell in the presence of God the Father, to fulfill every promise made by God to man. Calling back to what we discussed above, Jesus "is the author and finisher of our faith."

We must trust in the word of God made flesh, and in every word that comes from the mouth of God. There is a perfect symmetry for us to follow. We must fully and explicitly follow Jesus, trusting that He is the only path to eternal life. As we learn that, we learn that every word that God has spoken to His prophets, and every word that He speaks to our hearts through the Holy Spirit, is likewise our only path to our promised land. The words are our directions for traveling on the Journey of Faith. The words are our light for following the path that God prepares for us. The words of God guide us as we learn and obey them, and the Word of God leads us as we learn of Him and follow Him.

Let's go back to the discussion of the father and the centurion by again reflecting on their professions of faith. The father, struggling with faith, said he believed, and then pleaded "help thou mine unbelief" (Mark 9:24). The centurion said, "speak the word only, and my servant shall be healed" (Matthew 8:8). After reviewing these stories, we may begin to identify a little more with the father than we would like, but we are unsure how to be more like the centurion. I think it requires training on our part. The following story teaches us something we can use to train our minds and our hearts to exercise greater faith.

Let's go back to the book of Ether and this time discuss the faith of the brother of Jared. Recall from the subsection "How the Lord Deals with His Children" that the brother of Jared had three questions about his barges and how his people were going to be able to use them to cross the sea. One of the things that came from that discussion was that the Lord wanted the brother of Jared to come up with a solution to the fact that there was no light in the vessels (see Ether 2).

With that charge, the brother of Jared went back and made some stones, which apparently were some kind of crystals that he made, because he said he had molten them out of the rock. Then he took his offerings and went to present his solution to the Lord. Ether 3 says: "Now behold, O Lord, and do not be angry with thy servant because of his weakness before thee; for we know . . . that we are unworthy before thee; because of the fall our natures have become evil continually; nevertheless, O Lord, thou hast given us a commandment that we must call upon thee, that from thee we may receive according to our desires. . . . O Lord, look upon me in pity, and turn away thine anger from this thy people, . . . behold these things which I have molten out of the rock. And I know, O Lord, that thou hast all power, and can do whatsoever thou wilt for the benefit of man; therefore touch these stones, O Lord, with thy finger, and prepare them that they may shine forth in darkness. . . . Behold, O Lord, thou canst do this" (Ether 3:2–5).

Like the father and the centurion, we see the tone of a man who feels unworthy of God. But just like the centurion who was sure that his desires would come to pass if Jesus would "speak the word only," the brother of Jared states: "Behold, O Lord, thou canst do this." No matter how inadequate we may feel about ourselves, when we understand and know that God has power to fulfill His promises, we can still exercise great faith. Whenever you are faced with a difficulty, look to the examples in scripture where the Lord has revealed His hand. Do any scripture accounts feel similar to your situation? Any account that feels similar to your situation can serve as evidence for you that the Lord is able to provide the thing you hope for (help or deliverance or blessing).

The power of scripture is the power of the word of God, and the power of the Spirit. As you study scripture stories, you can feel the Spirit testifying that the Lord has that power still. Thus, you will have assurance and evidence, which are the elements from which faith is produced. Remind yourself as often as you need that the Lord can do this, and allow it to help your faith grow. Reminding ourselves that the Lord can do "this" (whatever thing requires our faith) has another effect as well. It reminds us that faith ultimately is centered on the will of God.

I had the experience of serving as a missionary in Brazil. During that time, I felt that I worked hard, but I did not feel like my efforts were rewarded. My mission president told me that I needed to work with more faith. I remember wondering what that meant and asking him to explain faith to me. Among other things, he told me that faith is an expectation. I knew then that I did not understand what he meant, and it took me years before I felt I understood it. In my mind, I did have an expectation, which is why I worked hard. But the problem was that the expectation I had was that my work would bring to pass what I wanted. I had an expectation of what results and what reward I wanted for my work, and then I worked as hard as I could to obtain them. While it frustrated me at the time that things didn't work out how I wanted, as I look back it is not surprising things didn't work out.

What I think about the expectation of faith now is very different from what I thought then. As I said, back then I thought the expectation of faith was that my work, my effort, would make something happen that I wanted to have happen. After all, what I wanted was to bring good things to the people I served, so I felt that I wanted a good thing. What I think my mission president was trying to teach me was that expectation is about my confidence in the Lord's words and that the Lord is able to do *His* work. I have confidence that He has power, and I trust that He has wisdom. When I have that confidence and that trust, I expect the Lord's will to be done to carry out His words, no matter what else may happen.

So where does that put my effort? Let's go back and reflect on the story of the brother of Jared that we just reviewed. He obviously put out effort in molting the sixteen small stones/crystals from the rock. However, he did not expect his effort alone to produce something that could give light to the ships. Rather, it was never about his effort. He presented those "things" so that the Lord would touch them with His finger to make them shine. The brother of Jared expected that if he would put in his effort to make those crystals, God would help with what he could not do, and cause them to shine. Expectation in faith does not come from our effort, but in our confidence that the Lord can do anything He desires to bring about His will. Our effort shows our dedication and commitment to do the word and will of God. Our effort shows that we want to be in the right place at the right time, giving all we have so that the Lord can bless us. We trust that our efforts will put us where the Lord can bring about miracles, whether small or great. The brother of Jared took his stones/crystals to the Lord, knowing that he himself did not know how to make something glow. He provided his effort specifically to be touched by the Lord's hand to bring about the Lord's will, to do the Lord's work.

I wonder what I could have done during my missionary service if I had better understood this. I try to apply this understanding of the Definition of Faith to my life now so that my Journey of Faith takes me to the Lord's promised land for me. My expectation now is centered in the idea that "Behold, O Lord, thou canst do this," and knowing that I can look to the word of God to guide me along the path.

As we come to the end of this section, let's attempt to recap what we've learned. God is trustworthy, and there are a lot of witnesses to that fact. When we hear the word of God, we need to let it spark our souls so we can stir up the courage to put His word to the test by action in our own lives, obeying the Lord's words. We do that by generating desire: desire to know, and desire to obtain the promises, and desire to be faithful on our part. As we do, we patiently hope for His word to be fulfilled in our lives, and we eventually find that every promise He has ever made will come to pass (although not necessarily as we expected or on the timeline we desire). He will guide us to what is best, and as we accept His will, we will either come to understand His will or we will feel peace that even though we cannot understand it, everything is for our good. This process helps us understand the Definition of Faith, and is there for all of us to follow. It doesn't matter where we are starting, or if we are starting over, as long as we feel a strong enough desire to begin the experiment.

NOTES

1. Dennis E. Simmons, "But If Not . . ." *Ensign*, May 2004.
2. Incidentally, there is a very interesting article that discusses this: "What Does the Word 'Faith' Mean? What Is True Faith?" biblepages.net, accessed October 6, 2017, http://www.biblepages.net/nba091.htm.

FEELING *of* FAITH

Imagine I show you some exercise equipment—something relatively small that was purchased after watching a late-night infomercial. Maybe you have some you could show me. It's so inspiring to buy that equipment so that we can have the same sort of change-our-fitness experiences that we see on the sales pitch. But how easy is it, really, to end up like one of the people in the testimonials? Personal experience tells me that it is clearly the exception rather than the rule.

If we know that we want to have better fitness and we buy the equipment or program that promises to make it happen, why is it so hard to sustain an exercise program that will give us real results? I think one of the keys is that sustained fitness is more than doing exercise, even if we are following a routine. The fact is that if we hate the exercise we are doing, we will eventually (and likely very quickly) burn out, and it will not do us any good. But similarly, if we get excited enough about fitness to buy the exercise equipment and then never use it, that isn't going to do us any good either.

My wife and I got convinced to buy something off a late-night fitness infomercial, which then sat unused for some time. I eventually got interested in it and proceeded to follow the program for several months. I never did end up looking like any of the people on the videos, but I actually noticed better fitness because of sustained effort on that program. I think I stuck to the program because it was challenging enough to push me and yet enjoyable enough to keep my interest, and I felt better when I stuck to the program. What I learned is that we will actually sustain something when we *feel* what we *do* and when what we *do* inspires how we *feel*.

Similarly, to sustain real faith we need to feel something and we need to do something. Faith, then, is partly what we do and partly what we feel. The "do" is just as we've talked about up to this point: it is the action that is the manifestation of our trust and belief. But what does faith feel like? There might be many ways of describing it, but I am going to set out what I will refer to as the "four C's" of the Feeling of Faith: Courage, Confidence, Commitment, and Comfort. Of course, we could order those four any way we like. I ordered them based on the scripture story of the stripling warriors from the book of Alma in the Book of Mormon, which I think highlights each one.

Let's recall the story of these young men who go to war and compare it to our own lives as we try to apply our faith to go to war against darkness. In Alma 53, we read that a group of people called the people of Ammon were about to break a covenant they had made that they would never again take up their weapons of war. Notice that the reason they wanted to break their covenant was for a good cause—many were dying on the battlefield to protect them, and surely they could have thought that it was justifiable to take up arms to defend those that were defending them at the cost of their own lives. It could be argued that their covenant and subsequent exodus was what started the war anyway. And after all, what is the sense in covenanting to not take up arms and instead be willing to lay down your own life, only to watch as others defend you to the death?

Faith in this story starts right at the very beginning. Helaman and his brethren were absolutely certain that the Lord wanted the people to keep their covenant, to the point they convinced the people of Ammon to step away from the war. I imagine a scene from a movie dramatization where Helaman comes in to talk to one of the more outspoken of the covenant-makers considering becoming a covenant-breaker, as he is strapping on his armor. The man says, "We cannot let them suffer and die for us like this when we are capable of doing our part!" "This is not your war to fight," Helaman would say to this man. "The Lord led us to where we are. Let's allow Him to carry us through." The man's son would then come up behind them and offer that he did not make that covenant. Then he would ask for his father's armor to go in the place of his father to honor the Nephites who fought on their behalf, as well as honoring his own family and people. I think that would be a good scene!

Returning to the actual scriptural account in Alma 56, Helaman wrote in his epistle to Captain Moroni, who headed up the army, that "I would not suffer them that they should break this covenant which they had made, supposing that God would strengthen us, insomuch that we should not suffer more because of the fulfilling the oath which they had taken" (Alma 56:8). We see that Helaman trusted that "God would strengthen" them so that those who had made covenants could keep them. The example of the faith of their leader, Helaman, seems a very appropriate starting point as we read about the faith of the stripling warriors, or the sons of this people, whom Helaman ends up leading into war. Let's also remember in our own lives the faith of Helaman: the Lord will strengthen and bless us for being faithful, especially in the face of what seems like justification to make an exception. In light of that, let's address the "four C's" of the Feeling of Faith. As we do, consider how each one is a feeling to accompany the actions of faith that will motivate us and keep us moving forward, just as we need to "feel" the exercise to continue with a selected exercise routine.

Courage

In Alma 53, Helaman tells us this about the young men who had agreed to go to war under his leadership: "And they were all young men, and they were exceedingly valiant for courage, and also for strength and activity; but behold, this was not all—they were men who were true at all times in whatsoever thing they were entrusted. Yea, they were men of truth and soberness, for they had been taught to keep the commandments of God and to walk uprightly before him" (Alma 53:20–21). These were young men who were "exceedingly valiant for courage" and "true at all times." The expression "exceedingly valiant for courage" is an interesting phrase and introduces us to the Feeling of Faith. The expression "true at all times" is one I understand as being associated with trustworthiness, which we will recall from above is related to the root word translated into English as "faith." These young men were the epitome of faithfulness or trustworthiness—"true at all times in whatsoever thing they were entrusted." The verse also identifies them as "exceedingly valiant . . . for strength and activity."

I believe the concepts of faithfulness, strength, and activity are related to, or perhaps integral to, courage. Surely anyone who has felt courage understands the connection between courage and activity. I think courage is always shown in action, and you cannot show courage without taking action (even if that action is the act of self-control or choosing not to act). While we can understand that activity is a hallmark of courage, the important question is this: What motivates the feeling of courage, the kind of feeling that will make us valiant to activity? We'll try to answer that question by seeing if we can figure out why these young men felt such courage. That can help us understand how that feeling of courage relates to faith.

This army of young men, untrained and inexperienced in battle, joined forces with the army of Antipus, which was in desperate need of reinforcements. After some time and training, the young men are to be used as a decoy in a strategy to get the Lamanites to leave their stronghold and fight on open ground. They are the bait, and the Lamanite army takes it, following after them to destroy them. The stripling warriors pick up the pace of their retreat so as to not be overtaken by the Lamanites. Then the army of Antipus comes up behind the Lamanites. We see the stripling warriors continuing to race forward, with the Lamanites in pursuit, and the army of Antipus in pursuit of them. The Lamanite army eventually stops.

At this point, Helaman asks the young men what they want to do, because surely if the Lamanites were stopping, the army of Antipus would catch up to them if they hadn't already. In Alma 56:44–45, we read: "Therefore what say ye, my sons, will ye go against them to battle? And now I say unto you, my beloved brother Moroni, that never had I seen so great courage, nay, not amongst all the Nephites." The source of their courage is identified a couple verses later: “Now they never had fought, yet they did not fear death; and they did think more upon the liberty of their fathers than they did upon their lives; yea, they had been taught by their mothers, that if they did not doubt, God would deliver them” (Alma 56:47). There are three components here that to me define courage and identify reasons for faith: first, “they did not fear death”; second, “they did think more upon the liberty of their fathers than they did upon their lives”; and, third, “they had been taught by their mothers, that if they did not doubt, God would deliver them.” Let’s look at each one in turn.

If you went to war, what do you think most people would tell you would be the worst-case personal scenario? My guess is that most people would consider the worst-case personal scenario of war to be the fact that you can die. What is the worst-case scenario for being completely honest at school—that you could lose friends? What about for standing up for what you believe at work—is the worst-case scenario that you could be fired? What if you didn’t fear the worst-case scenario? Maybe we could instead ask: What if you feared God more than you feared the worst-case scenario? What if you believed that God would take care of you even in the face of the worst-case scenario?

I think about my own life to try to decide when I would not fear the worst-case scenario. I think I do not fear the worst-case scenario when some other outcome is more important to me than the worst-case scenario. When I can be mentally prepared for the worst-case scenario ahead of time, I can overcome my fear of it. My courage increases when my fear decreases, and a lack of fear comes from accepting that even if the worst-case scenario happens, everything will somehow work out or everything will be right. Remember the Focus of Faith and Shadrach, Meshach, and Abed-nego.

Getting back to our story, we can reason that the stripling warriors did not fear death because they had a vision of a bigger picture and focused on something else instead. Namely, "they did think more upon the liberty of their fathers" than upon their own lives, which is the second component of courage. These young men gave up their own will for the benefit of others. They gave up their will because of their vision of the bigger picture. Likewise, when we are willing to give up our own will so that God's wisdom and power can be shown, we will find greater courage to be faithful to His words. We'll stop focusing all our energy on preserving our lives and our desires, and we'll be more willing to experience whatever the Lord wants of us.

The third component of courage brings us back full circle. We will not fear when we have no doubt that everything will work out in the best way possible for all of God's children as a whole. We'll accept the experience of our Trial of Faith as we understand that this life is but a small part of our eternal nature, and we trust that God will deliver our ultimate goals if we try to stay on His path. In fact, I would suggest that building up courage works best when we place our doubts and fears to the side and act on a selfless motivation. This is, after all, the example that Jesus Christ provided for us. These young men exemplified the same courage we will need to feel to be able to exercise our faith: feeling our trust enough to act faithfully in the face of every challenge.

Confidence

I consider confidence and courage to be slight variations of each other. Confidence typically prepares us to have courage, as seen in the story that follows. However, I also think that if we can build up enough courage to do something, we will begin to feel confidence. We can think of courage as feeling the motivation and power to be able to stand up against challenges, and confidence as feeling assurance that our thoughts and acts are trustworthy. Here's that word *assurance* again that we looked at in Hebrews 11.

Picking up where Helaman asks these young men if they are willing to engage the Lamanites in battle, he reports in Alma 56:46 that their response was, "Father, behold our God is with us, and he will not suffer that we should fall; then let us go forth; we would not slay our brethren if they would let us alone; therefore let us go, lest they should overpower the army of Antipus." Then we continue with verse 47, which we already looked at: "Now they never had fought, yet they did not fear death; and they did think more upon the liberty of their fathers than they did upon their lives; yea, they had been taught by their mothers, that if they did not doubt, God would deliver them." And finally we see in verse 48 that "they rehearsed unto me the words of their mothers, saying: We do not doubt our mothers knew it."

So why did they have courage? Because they had great confidence in what they had been taught. They *felt sure*, which is really the definition of assurance after all, that their mothers knew. Even if they did not yet know for themselves, they were sure their mothers knew. Our faith also frequently begins based on feeling sure of the testimony of others (or our own testimony of previous things), and feeling assurance that God will do His part, just as these young men were sure that God would deliver them if they did not doubt. So we can define courage by how we act when we overcome doubt, and confidence by the feelings that help us overcome doubt.

Commitment

If you are familiar with the story of the stripling warriors, you know that the young men went into battle, were victorious, and not a single one of them was killed. Later in the account of these young men they end up in another battle. They again win this battle without any of the young men being killed. This time Helaman gives a little more insight into what kind of soldiers they were, which gives us a little more insight into how faith works. In Alma 57:21, Helaman says: "Yea, and they did obey and observe to perform every word of command with exactness; yea, and even according to their faith it was done unto them; and I did remember the words which they said unto me that their mothers had taught them."

I have always loved that verse. However, I am not sure I had a good sense for what this verse was about. I think I used to equate faith with obedience and hard work. But I have come to realize that faith is not a straight equivalent to obedience. And while hard work is necessary in many aspects of life, it doesn't in itself inform us whether a person has the kind of faith we're talking about. Let's dig a little deeper into this verse to see why. I think the expressions "every word of command" and "with exactness" apply to both "obey" and to "observe to perform." So we can expand out the language of the verse to say: "they did obey every word of command with exactness and they did observe to perform every word of command with exactness." At first glance we might think these phrases are redundant. However, I believe that when the Lord wanted the scriptures to be redundant, He inspired His servants to use the same language for effect. In those cases the redundancy has a message separate from the message itself. When the Lord inspired His servants to use different language that sounds similar, I believe it is not a matter of redundancy, but a different message.

To me, the first phrase most clearly refers to obedience, seeing that it says they did *obey* every word of command with exactness. The message is one of strict obedience. That is related to what we do. That's like following the exercise program that comes with the exercise equipment so that we accomplish what it was designed for. The second phrase gives me more of the impression of intention of these young men. That's like getting into the exercise routines and dedicating ourselves to them. The scripture says they did "observe to perform . . . with exactness." They did not just obey with exactness, but they "observed to perform," meaning they carefully went about doing what they were doing. They paid attention to what they were doing and measured their actions to make sure to achieve strict obedience. There is a measured intention about their exact obedience—not likely from fear or habit, but from intention to do what was expected of them. Why does their intention matter? Helaman gives us the answer at the end of the verse: "I did remember the words which they said unto me that their mothers had taught them." They obeyed with the intention of faith. We could say that they obeyed with the Eye of Faith, as discussed in the next section. They knew the promises the Lord had made, and they put forth the effort they believed was required to obtain them, or perhaps said better: to prepare themselves to receive them.

Doesn't that describe commitment? We can say these young were committed to what their mothers had taught them, so much so that they observed to perform every word of command with exactness to receive the promised blessings. I suppose someone could argue that *commitment* and *conviction* are just synonyms for the word *belief*. However, everyone I have known that could be described as having commitment or conviction has been a person that feels something deeply rooted. There is firmness to their commitment. The commitment of faith is something more. It is when we feel committed to the process of exercising faith and the "things hoped for," as well as committed to achieving the outcome of our faith. This is what the young men were—committed to whatever they needed to do.

I talked about serving as a missionary in Brazil and having my mission president tell me to work with more faith, which he told me was an expectation of the good things we hope for. I still struggled, though, because I put out effort intending to fulfill my purposes. After months went by, that mission president finished his service and a new mission president came out to serve. I ended up in a conversation with the new mission president over much the same subject matter—why didn't I see things happening when I worked so hard? He opened the scriptures to answer my questions. We read the following from Alma 26: "Behold, the field was ripe, and blessed are ye, for ye did thrust in the sickle, and did reap with your might, yea, all the day long did ye labor; and behold the number of your sheaves! And they shall be gathered into the garners, that they are not wasted. Yea, they shall not be beaten down by the storm at the last day; yea, neither shall they be harrowed up by the whirlwinds; but when the storm cometh they shall be gathered together in their place, that the storm cannot penetrate to them; yea, neither shall they be driven with fierce winds whithersoever the enemy listeth to carry them. But behold, they are in the hands of the Lord of the harvest, and they are his; and he will raise them up at the last day" (Alma 26:5–7).

I admit that I did not see what significance these verses had to the question of why I wasn't seeing more success. I reasoned that these verses explained exactly why I should have been seeing success, which raised further confusion why I wasn't seeing the success of my labor. As these thoughts went through my head, my mission president pointed me to review verse 7 again. He said something along these lines: "It says that '*he* will raise them up at the last day.' Not you. It isn't your job to raise them up; it is the Lord's!" I never did realize during my missionary service that two separate mission presidents in two distinct ways had given me the same answer to the same question. It wasn't until years later that I connected the similarities of these two conversations.

I think the first mission president wanted me to exercise faith in that he wanted me to stop focusing so much on my work as the solution and focus instead on work as the means to the Lord's promised blessings. As with the commitment of the stripling warriors, I could commit to the work with my intention of serving the Lord and His children. Instead, I had tried to obtain my desires through work, or simply through my own efforts. I needed to serve the Lord with work to exercise faith that He would take care of things. I hope I am expressing that point well, because I am sure I am not the only person who has struggled with it. I now try to make sure that my efforts and my work are my offering to the Lord in faith—not that I will do it all but as a showing of my commitment.

My second mission president said much the same thing, identifying the fact that I was supposed to be engaged in the Lord's work and I needed to remember that it was His work and it is His purposes that I should be trying to fulfill. I realize looking back that I spent a lot of effort trying to drag the Lord to where I wanted to go, and I could have done a better job of turning my effort over to Him and allowing Him to guide me. In short, my commitment was to the work I thought I should be doing, instead of fully committing to doing the Lord's work. We can have a similar change of focus in our work and acts of faith. The difference is in how you are committed or where your intention is—whether you commit to do your thing and hope it pleases the Lord, as opposed to committing yourself to the Lord and trusting He will bless you in what you need and desire. The second approach is really the faith approach. As I have tried to live those principles, I feel that my efforts are more efforts of faith.

So how does the commitment of faith work? Let's read a little more about what Helaman says about these young men. After the second battle, he reports the following in Alma 57: "And it came to pass that there were two hundred, out of my two thousand and sixty, who had fainted because of the loss of blood; nevertheless, according to the goodness of God, and to our great astonishment, and also the joy of our whole army, there was not one soul of them who did perish; yea, and neither was there one soul among them who had not received many wounds. And now, their preservation was astonishing to our whole army, yea, that they should be spared while there was a thousand of our brethren who were slain. And we do justly ascribe it to the miraculous power of God, because of their exceeding faith in that which they had been taught to believe—that there was a just God, and whosoever did not doubt, that they should be preserved by his marvelous power. Now this was the faith of these of whom I have spoken; they are young, and their minds are firm, and they do put their trust in God continually" (Alma 57:25–27).

Their faith was that whosoever did not doubt should be preserved by the power of God. Verse 27 then indicates that "their minds are firm, and they do put their trust in God continually." I think this helps identify how they could "not doubt": their commitment to God was so strong they continually trusted in Him. They committed themselves to the Lord's will and trusted He would do with them what was best.

Comfort

One more point that the account of the stripling warriors helps illustrate about faith is the feeling of comfort that accompanies faith. In Alma 57, Helaman finishes giving an account of how he saw the Lord's hand in the preservation of the people. He says "I was filled with exceeding joy because of the goodness of God in preserving us, that we might not all perish; yea, and I trust that the souls of them who have been slain have entered into the rest of their God" (Alma 57:36). He first recognizes the hand of the Lord in preserving the Nephites. When we exercise true faith as we have been discussing, the result of our faith is manifested and we feel a greater assurance because of it. There is a comfort in having your trust confirmed.

But there is more, because Helaman's people lost a great number of soldiers to the war. Although the people as a whole were preserved by the hand of the Lord, many still died. How often do the results of our faith come in exactly the manner we hoped for? The greater the trial, the more likely there will be significant things along the way that will not turn out according to our desires. And while there is comfort in knowing our faith was rewarded, perhaps the greater comfort comes as we can recognize that the results of our faith came despite what did not go the way we would have liked. To me the greater comfort is in being able to identify all the challenges we faced, and to realize that despite so many things going "the wrong way," the Lord's hand was actually guiding us every step of the way. Surely not one of the surviving Nephite soldiers would take pleasure in the loss of those souls who fought with them, but they could take comfort that their brethren were doing what they were supposed to be doing the whole time. Likewise, we can trust we are in a better place for the apparently negative things that pushed, redirected, and took us through to seeing our faith confirmed.

This comfort that we feel in faith is the surest path to greater faith. Faith is generally built by reflection as we review what we have experienced, and see that the Lord came through for us. Those who seek for signs seek for the extraordinary, and miss the peaceful comfort that true trust in the Lord brings.

The "four C's" are really about turning our hearts to God through faith. Our heart is what we generally associate with our feelings. It defines how we are going to act, and what motivates us to act as we do. It is what gets us up off the couch to do our exercise routine, and it is what gets us up off of our doubt and fear to exercise faith. Courage and confidence predict that we will stand for right, whatever challenges face us. We are going to act on our trust because we have overcome our doubt and fear by a burning desire for the blessing of the Lord. Commitment and comfort motivate us to action, because we have set our hearts on something greater than ourselves, and we trust that even when things do not go the way we would choose, we know the Lord will take us to a better place. We act, looking forward to the power of the Lord's hand helping and guiding us along, and we reflect looking backward to see that God is faithful and consistent. When we feel these things, we will act on what we believe. They are the Feeling of Faith.

May we each commit ourselves to seeking the Lord's will, and have the courage to act on that commitment. As we do, we'll feel confidence in our own efforts, as well as perfect confidence that the Lord will come through for us. We'll be comforted by the peace of the Lord as we act to take the path we feel we should be on, trusting the Lord to lead us to the best outcome.

EYE *of* FAITH

LET'S TALK FOR A MOMENT ABOUT MUSTARD. FOR ANY WHO have read the Gospels, you might think that any extensive discussion about faith needs to reference mustard seeds at some point to be complete. So, let's talk about mustard seeds.

Look at this dot: •

That dot is approximately the size or diameter of a mustard seed, and maybe a little bigger than some mustard seeds. The mustard seed is so small as to practically be insignificant to us (usually about 1–2 mm in diameter). If you had a handful of mustard seeds and one fell out of your hand, it would surprise me if you even noticed. But a mustard seed the size of that dot has the capability to grow into a mustard plant. While most mustard plants are not necessarily what we think of as a "tree," but maybe a bush, they grow large enough for birds to land in them, and there are some mustard plants that can grow even as tall as a grown man.

Jesus used the image of a mustard seed on a couple of occasions. One was when He drew the analogy of the seed of mustard to the kingdom of heaven in Matthew 13:31–32, "The kingdom of heaven is like to a grain of mustard seed, which a man took, and sowed in his field: Which indeed is the least of all seeds: but when it is grown, it is the greatest among herbs, and becometh a tree, so that the birds of the air come and lodge in the branches thereof." This parable was not about faith, but it provides interesting background into what Jesus expected people understood about mustard. Namely, mustard starts out as the smallest of seeds and yet grows to the greatest tree among herbs. It has amazing potential for growth: to go from being insignificant to something substantial.

In light of that understanding, let's look at another place where Jesus is recorded to have mentioned the mustard seed. In Matthew 17:20, where He answers the question by His disciples about why they could not cast the devil out of a child, we read: "And Jesus said unto them, Because of your unbelief: for verily I say unto you, If ye have faith as a grain of mustard seed, ye shall say unto this mountain, Remove hence to yonder place; and it shall remove; and nothing shall be impossible unto you." Another version of these teachings is found in Luke 17:6, which states: "And the Lord said, If ye had faith as a grain of mustard seed, ye might say unto this sycamine tree, Be thou plucked up by the root, and be thou planted in the sea; and it should obey you."

Notice that the verse in Matthew talks about removing a mountain, while the verse in Luke talks about moving a sycamore tree (or sycamine tree in the older English of the KJV Bible). In both verses, we see that it is the *quality* of the seed, rather than the size of the seed, that will determine whether the desired result will be obtained. Perhaps we could say the quality of the seed determines whether a tree of faith will grow. Recall the significance of a good seed from our discussion above in the Definition of Faith. Recall also that we plant a seed of faith and nourish it to grow it into a tree. Whether our faith seed is insignificant or not even noticeable at first, it has significant growth potential if we will nurture it.

While the message of the quality of the seed is a powerful one, I think that is not the only message. We can learn another powerful message from these verses that accompanies the message of the quality of the seed. Notice that in both the account in Matthew as well as the account in Luke, there is the use of the word *this*, as in "ye shall say unto *this* mountain" and "ye might say unto *this* sycamine tree." I imagine that these lessons taught by the Savior were done in context. I imagine that when Jesus taught these messages, He was likely on a mountain with the disciples when He told them "ye shall say unto *this* mountain," or perhaps He pointed to a large tree and told them "ye might say unto *this* sycamine tree."

I think the message of faith is that it is specific and focused, as well as being pure. By this point in time I hope we can all understand that faith is not simply some vague feeling or ethereal concept. Faith is concrete enough to produce action on our part, as long as we are committed and courageous enough to act. The Eye of Faith is focused on the objective of our faith, or what we hope will come to pass. We need to have an eye specific to the task at hand when we exercise faith. We can have all the faith in the world that the Lord will answer our prayers, but if we lack faith and understanding that the Lord would like us to love and serve our neighbor, we will not likely exercise much faith or make much effort to look for opportunities to do that. Consequently, we would probably never see the blessings such faith would bring.

Let's get back to the seed. If we spread a whole field full of tiny mustard seeds, we shouldn't expect to get an olive tree or a sycamore tree. The type and quality of the seed will lead to the fruit of that faith. Recall the analogy by Alma, in that it is the process of exercising faith that turns a seed into a fruit-bearing tree. And that tree with fruit on it represents the sure knowledge and multiplied blessings that come from our cultivating our seed of faith and our subsequent tree of faith. He refers to a perfect knowledge "in that thing" in which we exercised faith (see Alma 32:31–34). We need to fill our lives or our field of faith with all different kinds of seeds and all different varieties of trees. Invariably, some will be saplings while others are closer to maturing and yet others may not even be planted yet. I believe it is expected to be a lifetime of work.

Pure faith applied to specific challenges and issues will allow us to move specific mountains or perform specific miracles the Lord would have us do. Purity in faith, or the quality of the seed, comes from the sincerity of the intent or the focus of the commitment we apply to the process of exercising faith. The idea of purity of faith deals with how committed we actually are to seeking and understanding the truth and obtaining the outcome the Lord would desire. But what does it mean to apply our faith specifically?

Magnifying Our Efforts

Let's start to answer that question by talking about a magnifying glass. If we were to hold up a magnifying glass on a sunny day, we could hold it at just the right angle at just the right distance to produce a very bright spot on something. The bright spot will be much smaller in diameter than the diameter of the magnifying glass. The magnifying glass acts as a lens in that circumstance, where the photons or energy particles that make up the light are redirected and focused by the magnifying glass. Instead of the photons landing spread out on the ground or paper or whatever else we put under the magnifying glass, all the photons over the entire area of the magnifying glass are redirected to intersect at the bright spot we produce. The effect of the redirection of the light is a concentration of photons over a much smaller area.

The concentration of photons intersecting at the same point causes all the energy of all those photons to be focused on that particular point. Focusing all the energy to the particular point enables us to produce a lot more heat than if we left the light spread out over the entire area of the magnifying glass. All the heat and energy that would have been spread out is now in one small area. If we focus that light on some target like a piece of paper or wood, we can produce enough heat to start a fire, whereas otherwise the energy would be spread over the larger area, and would not produce enough heat to light a fire.

In this example, the magnifying glass is our Eye of Faith. When we spread a few thoughts and scatter some of our feeling and dedication over a subject, we may never achieve the desired outcome of our faith. We simply cannot expect to generate much spiritual energy where we put little thought and minimal effort. However, when we focus our thoughts and put the whole feeling of our heart into the will of the Lord and the outcome promised by Him, we can move a mountain, or a sycamore tree, or do whatever else the Lord would have us do. We can produce enough energy to ignite a spiritual fire within ourselves.

Let's look at Ether 12:19, where we read: "And there were many whose faith was so exceedingly strong, even before Christ came, who could not be kept from within the veil, but truly saw with their eyes the things which they had beheld with an eye of faith, and they were glad." Did you see what he says about the exercise of faith? When our faith is strong enough and focused enough, we will *truly see with our eyes the things which we have beheld with the Eye of Faith*. Now let's recall some of our discussion from above, and go all the way back to the first account we read, where Nephi committed to doing whatever the Lord wanted of him. He knew he was supposed to get the plates. He knew that the Lord had promised to deliver Laban into his hands, and deliver him the plates. But he had no idea how any of that was supposed to happen. Still, his faith was strong, and his mind's eye was focused on obeying the Lord and achieving the promised outcome. And so he went up not knowing how the Lord would accomplish His purposes, but trying to follow the Spirit, relying upon acting on what he saw with the Eye of Faith instead of whatever doubts or questions may have presented themselves (see 1 Nephi 4:6).

The magnifying glass focuses light to a specific point, which is a point fixed in space based on the incoming light and the design of the magnifying glass. If we try to start a piece of paper on fire with that magnifying glass, we will find that if we hold the lens either too far away from the paper or too close to the paper, we will not focus the energy on the paper, and thus will not produce the heat necessary to start the fire. We focus with the Eye of Faith by envisioning in our mind's eye the Lord carrying out His word, even if we don't need to know exactly how He is going to do it.

The lens of our Eye of Faith should be like that magnifying glass, focusing on a specific point, which brings power to our efforts on the thing we focus on. Similar to how that magnifying glass has to be held at the right distance to focus to a specific point if we are going to light a fire, we need to keep the lens of our Eye of Faith at the right place to produce spiritual fire. When the magnifying glass is held too close, the lens can't focus on the object we wish to ignite. Similarly, the lens of our Eye of Faith can focus quickly with our initial enthusiasm for faith, only to have our faith dissipate as we try to focus on our desires instead of focusing specifically on what the Lord wants. When the magnifying glass is held too far away, the lens focuses the light, but then the light starts to dissipate again before reaching the target. Thus, the lens cannot ignite the fire on our target. Similarly, the lens of our Eye of Faith can fail to focus on the object of our hope when we lack dedication and commitment to carry through with the obedience and activity that show our faith. For the lens of the Eye of Faith, we need to make our focus the Focus of Faith. We need to focus on the Savior.

We can envision the outcome and walk the path while still leaving both the outcome and the path in the hands of the Lord. We do our part (that which we feel we have been led to do), and trust that the Lord will take care of the outcome. It is important to remember the final promise or the final outcome, and not just focus on each step of the path, or we risk getting caught up in our efforts. We do not need to do more than our part (like me as I was a missionary trying to do it all myself), and we cannot do less than our part (like passively waiting for the Lord to make things happen without commitment on our part), or we risk having the wrong focus. This is how we can be very focused and specific in our faith while not knowing how things will end up. Jesus did not say we needed to know what means would be used to move the mountain when we "say unto *this* mountain, Remove hence to yonder place" (Matthew 17:20).

When we see with the Eye of Faith, we will not try to tell the Lord how to run the universe, or even how to run our lives. Let Him decide how the mountain should be moved, and then do what He asks us to do, trusting that He will provide a way to move the mountain. We only need to focus specifically on which mountain will be moved and do what the Lord asks of us and all we feel is right. Much of the time the Lord will first help us identify the mountain, then He will await our focus and faith (our part, our action), and then He will act to make the mountain move. The most important thing we need to see in our mind's eye is that the mountain is gone.

I think some of this discussion can feel a little vague, especially when we consider that part of "seeing" with the Eye of Faith is refocusing and redirecting ourselves, which means acting on what we see in our mind's eye. One of the problems we run into as we try to apply this in our lives is that our ability to see is very limited and our willingness to act can be likewise limited. We do not understand things as God does, and cannot see with His perspective. And unless we try to elevate our thinking, we may not be able to envision the Lord's promised outcome with our Eye of Faith.

My more successful experiences in "seeing the mountain gone" have been when I have tried to imagine two things. The first is to imagine what things will look like with the mountain gone. If we are talking about an actual mountain, I could picture in my mind the landscape without the mountain in it. When we talk about specific challenges we face in life, I try to imagine what type of person I will be when that specific challenge is overcome, instead of just imaging my life without the challenge. I think imagining what I will be like when the challenge is overcome is much more powerful than trying to imagine not having the challenge any more. It is also more likely to be consistent with how the Lord deals with us, His children.

The second thing is to imagine what life will feel like with the mountain gone. I imagine what feelings I will have when I no longer have to struggle with that challenge. We can even tie this into the Feeling of Faith, and build on how those feelings will play into our lives post-challenge. I also allow myself to focus on the feelings I have already experienced struggling against it. I imagine what I will feel like doing once I stop focusing my energy on the challenge or on the problems I face. And then I try to start doing *now* the things I figure I would do with those feelings once the challenge is overcome, as though the challenge is already overcome. That way I can try to be the person I see in my mind who has already overcome the challenge.

Thy Faith Hath Made Thee Whole

Let's review the story of a woman who saw with the Eye of Faith. As we will see, she was a woman terribly afflicted. Yet she saw in her mind's eye the power of the Savior making her whole. And importantly, she acted on what she saw with an Eye of Faith, thus making her faith active. To get the full account of the woman I want to talk about, we have to intersect it with another scriptural account that comes before it, because I believe they are more powerful together.

In Luke 8:41–42, we read: "And, behold, there came a man named Jairus, and he was a ruler of the synagogue: and he fell down at Jesus' feet, and besought him that he would come into his house: For he had one only daughter, about twelve years of age, and she lay a dying. But as he went the people thronged him." This account of Jairus is really interesting in itself, but we're really reading it here to set up the scene for the woman's story. It's important to understand that there are a lot of people around Jesus as He is trying to make His way to the home of Jairus. The people *thronged* Jesus, meaning they crowded around. I think of leaving the stadium after a sports match—there are a lot of people trying to go the same direction, and some trying to go the other direction. You can't help but bump into each other or be pressed right against each other as you try to move.

It is against the backdrop of this scene that we encounter the woman: "And a woman having an issue of blood twelve years, which had spent all her living upon physicians, neither could be healed of any, Came behind him, and touched the border of his garment: and immediately her issue of blood stanched" (Luke 8:43–44). Before we continue with our story, we need to look back at Leviticus 15 to understand what we are reading here. Starting around verse 19, we read some prescriptions of how to handle the circumstance of a woman hemorrhaging blood (or having "an issue of blood"), which is often thought to refer to a woman's menstrual cycle. There was a required ceremonial separation and cleansing related to a woman's period. The main point we want to take away from this is in verse 25, which states: "*all the days of the issue* of her uncleanness shall be as the days of her separation: *she shall be unclean*" (emphasis added). A woman with an issue of blood is considered unclean under the Mosaic Law and the Jewish customs. Very importantly, when someone was considered unclean, they were restricted from gathering with groups of people.

So what we have here is a woman who is ceremonially unclean, and is thus not allowed to be in a group of people, such as this group of people crowding around Jesus. The worst part of this, of course, is the fact that the woman had the issue of blood for twelve years! Think of this for a moment to have a little understanding and compassion for this woman—for twelve years she had been effectively an outcast of society. She obviously would not have been allowed to attend religious services, the feasts and ceremonies, or anything else you might imagine wanting to participate in, because they all involved gatherings of people. Think of the stigma you would normally associate with lepers, and that is essentially the stigma this woman carried, but without the outward evidence of disease. She carried this privately.

Now let's jump to the same account in Matthew to learn something else about this story. Matthew 9:20–21 states: "And, behold, a woman, which was diseased with an issue of blood twelve years, came behind him, and touched the hem of his garment: For she said within herself, If I may but touch his garment, I shall be whole." Her faith was very specific: she saw with her Eye of Faith that all she would need to do is touch the hem of the cloak of Jesus, and she would be healed. She saw the mountain removed! She trusted to the extent that her entire focus was on getting to the Savior. The problem of course is that He always seemed to be thronged with people, and she was ceremonially unclean, and thus by custom was not allowed to approach Him.

Her faith teaches us an important lesson—that we should not let anything get between us and what we see in our mind's eye or with an Eye of Faith to overcome our challenges. We should not let anything prevent us from approaching the Savior in faith. We see that so strong was her trust that she was rewarded immediately, and felt the issue of blood dry up.

As we talk about our mind's eye, I cannot help but think of Luke 11:34, where we read: "The light of the body is the eye: therefore when thine eye is single, thy whole body also is full of light; but when thine eye is evil, thy body also is full of darkness." Recalling something else that we have already seen, James 1:8 says he that wavers in his faith is a "double-minded" man. I believe that in contrast, someone who focuses the mind's eye (so someone whose "eye is single") is quite the opposite from a double-minded man, and will be a person of great faith with a very firm trust in the Lord. Jesus told us in Luke 11:34 that our whole bodies will be filled with light when our eye is single. Alma 32:34–35 tells us that the word (the seed of faith) swells our souls and expands our minds and that we can discern of its goodness because it is light. Our tiny seed, focused on the Lord's will, and envisioning the Lord fulfilling His word, is light for our entire body. Even a tiny seed of pure faith, coupled with the Eye of Faith, provides light to our whole soul and moves us to action and moves us to come to Christ. It can grow into the greatest of herbs within us.

In our times of challenge that light can be difficult to see. When a new challenge comes along requiring the exercise of our faith, we are once again thrust to the outer edge of the light that we perceive, and we must learn to focus our faith in new ways. President Boyd K. Packer taught that "Somewhere in your quest for spiritual knowledge, there is that 'leap of faith', as the philosophers call it. It is the moment when you have gone to the edge of the light and stepped into the darkness to discover that the way is lighted ahead for just a footstep or two."[1]The exercise of faith requires us to step into the darkness, or the unknown. If we knew for certain what was going to happen, it would not take any trust for us to carry on. But even when we are sure that the Lord will deliver us in the end, it is difficult to leave our comfort, and it can be downright frightening to experiment with the unknown.

The Vision of Faith that we talked about earlier is frequently something we only "see" with our hearts as we feel after the right path. We may be required to feel after that path by stepping out into the darkness. Sometimes we will wander by the light of faith for some time before we find the destination of our faith. We may plant a tiny seed and have to carefully cultivate it for it to begin to grow. We look with the Eye of Faith to obtain the blessings of the Lord, and to see the seed of faith growing, in time, into a tree of testimony. The Eye of Faith keeps us focused on a goal we see with the Vision of Faith. I think part of the reason Ether 12:19 tells us that people "truly saw with their eyes the things which they had beheld with an eye of faith, *and they were glad*" (emphasis added) is that sometimes we look with the Eye of Faith for what seems a very long time before we truly see with our eyes the things which we beheld with the Eye of Faith. Glad indeed! Sometimes it will be all we can do to maintain focus (which might be the Focus of Faith!). When that fulfillment of our faith finally comes, our hearts and minds will expand almost to overflowing and we will finally taste the fruit of the tree that eventually grows from our seed of faith.

Now let's go back to the rest of the story of the woman with the issue of blood in Luke 8, or we could miss another lesson on faith. After she stealthily came up and touched Jesus's clothes through the crowd of people, "Jesus said, Who touched me? When all denied, Peter and they that were with him said, Master, the multitude throng thee and press thee, and sayest thou, Who touched me? And Jesus said, Somebody hath touched me: for I perceive that virtue is gone out of me" (Luke 8:45–46). We see that Jesus wanted the woman to own up to what she did, in front of everyone. The question I have had is, why? I used to think that Jesus wanted this woman to explain what had happened so that the crowd could hear her testimony of what Jesus had done for her.

Her testimony is told as follows: "And when the woman saw that she was not hid, she came trembling, and falling down before him, she declared unto him before all the people for what cause she had touched him, and how she was healed immediately" (Luke 8:47). Again, I used to think that testimony was for the crowd. I have also thought that her testimony might have been for herself, because when our faith is rewarded, it can provide an anchor to our soul in future times of trial and difficulty (see Ether 12:4).

Both of those things may be true. But there's something here that stands out to me more than either of these. Remember the setup to this story: Jairus has come to ask Jesus to heal his daughter whom he believes to be at the point of death, or as good as dead. The healing of Jairus's daughter from the dead created a much greater stir than the testimony of the woman with the issue of blood. After discussion of these stories with my wife, I have begun to think that Jesus wanted the woman to confess her story in front of the crowd at least partly for the sake of Jairus. Here is a man who asks Jesus to come *quickly* as his daughter is at the point of death, and he fears, maybe dead already, making it too late. Imagine his frustration as they have to push through the crowd. I can only imagine Jairus's panic and his haste to have the Savior act.

I imagine how I feel (and how I generally act) in a traffic jam when I have an appointment to keep (or a plane to catch), and none of those circumstances have been anywhere near life or death situations like Jairus faced. And yet in Jairus's haste, Jesus stopped to help the woman with the issue of blood. I can feel frustration on Jairus's behalf. Couldn't it wait? In this case, the woman had already waited so long—maybe Jesus could help Jairus's daughter and then come back to the woman? I can feel Jairus's anxiety as he was probably thinking, can we please hurry up before it's too late!? But that woman then testified to the crowd and to Jairus that she had waited twelve years for the blessings they had just witnessed. My wife pointed out to me that Jairus's daughter is said to be about *twelve years of age*, adding one more layer of interest to this account—the woman who Jesus stopped to help had been suffering from her affliction for the entire lifetime of Jairus's daughter, whom Jairus was so anxious to have Jesus come and help. Surely Jairus could wait long enough for the Lord to help another soul in need. Notice how these stories intersect to lead up to gaining confidence in the Lord. The woman was healed immediately, but after a long, long trial. I believe her confession about the way she was healed immediately could provide comfort to Jairus, who worried that Jesus would arrive too late. But the compassion he showed as He stopped to help this woman, and the power He displayed in healing her, can give assurance to those of us, who like Jairus, wait on the Lord sometimes with impatience. His miracles can be instantaneous, if it is His will and if we have sufficient faith like the woman. But even if Christ seems to come too late or we are impatient with His timing, He is in control. It is never too late; as Jesus told the crowd when he finally arrived to attend to Jairus's daughter: "She is not dead, but sleepeth" (Luke 8:52). The Eye of Faith sees with the Focus of Faith, and reminds us also that God has a bigger perspective than what we understand. Sometimes our focus is too narrow to satisfy the Lord's will.

Despite our limited ability to see from the proper perspective, the Lord is patient with us. And to see just how compassionate the Lord was, we hear His reply to the woman's testimony: "And he said unto her, Daughter, be of good comfort: thy faith hath made thee whole; go in peace" (Luke 8:48). It is interesting to note that just a few verses later in our account, Jesus invited Jairus to "Fear not: believe only, and she shall be made whole" (Luke 8:50). Sometimes the example of someone else's faith is just what we need to start seeing with our own Eye of Faith.

After waiting so long for the blessing, the woman with the issue of blood was rewarded as soon as she found the Savior.

The "immediately dried up" part shows us the power of Jesus to bless our faith. But let's not overlook how long she waited before the blessing was given. I imagine this woman long envisioned a life free of the issue of blood that afflicted her. She probably envisioned it with each new physician she visited. I have learned that things are frequently that way in my life—there are many times I have to wait what seems a long time before what I envision is actually brought to reality by the Lord. The Eye of Faith is primarily about the principles of focus and envisioning in our mind's eye. But the Eye of Faith also encompasses the principle of patience, so that we can maintain our faith no matter what happens.

Many times we hear and use the expression "wait on the Lord" to refer to the fact that our timeline for our expectations frequently does not align with God's timeline. Sometimes our expectations themselves do not even completely align with God's will, no matter what timeline we look at. What we have to remember is to seek God's will, not ours, and that what the Lord states will *always* come to pass, even if it takes longer than we wanted. Even if it takes longer than we thought we could last.

Whenever I have used a magnifying glass to start something on fire, I find that I have to work at holding it steady in the right place. I have to hold that lens in the right place for long enough to produce the right amount of focus to finally produce enough energy to start my fire. When we struggle in life to maintain our focus for long enough to generate the energy necessary to produce the desire of our faith, there is hope and comfort in knowing the Lord is always faithful.

In Isaiah 40, Isaiah speaks the word of God to His people Israel in their time of trial. Conditions were terrible, and it must have seemed as though their suffering would not end, and that the Lord would not hear their cries. In addressing their concerns, Isaiah, the prophet, starts by saying, "Comfort ye, comfort ye my people, saith your God" (Isaiah 40:1). He then discusses the greatness of God and the nothingness of man. He emphasizes the fact that the things of man are temporary, but the word and goodness of God endure. Take comfort, he tells us, in knowing that even though the Lord's timeline is different from ours, He is there.

And then Isaiah states the following: "Hast thou not known? hast thou not heard, that the everlasting God, the Lord, the Creator of the ends of the earth, fainteth not, neither is weary? there is no searching of his understanding. He giveth power to the faint; and to them that have no might he increaseth strength. Even the youths shall faint and be weary, and the young men shall utterly fall: But they that wait upon the Lord shall renew their strength; they shall mount up with wings as eagles; they shall run, and not be weary; and they shall walk, and not faint" (Isaiah 40:28–31). As a father who has raised young children, I am regularly surprised by the seemingly boundless energy of a toddler or young child, who doesn't want to move without running. And yet, the Lord pointed out through His prophet that "even the youths shall faint and be weary." And then affirms that "they that wait upon the Lord shall *renew* their strength."

It is interesting to me that the verse doesn't say we won't get tired; rather, it says we shall *renew* our strength. Rest assured that in exercising faith, and especially maintaining our Eye of Faith fixed upon the blessings of the Lord, we will grow weary and likely will grow faint at some point in time. We may even stumble and fall. We might keep coming back mentally to where we planted our seed of faith and wonder when the plant will start to grow. Or we might see a seedling that seems to grow painfully slowly and wonder if it will ever mature into a tree that will bear fruit. Just as we saw previously with Peter, when we take our focus off the Savior, we begin to sink. In those circumstances, just as with Peter, let us call out "Lord, save me!" and He will pull us up to again walk with Him on the water. He will renew us in faith.

There's one more account I want to review while we're discussing the subject of seeing with the Eye of Faith. Israel and Syria had a long history of conflict going back to accounts recorded in the Old Testament. In the book of Second Kings, we read in chapter 6 about the king of Syria trying to war against Israel, but failing to gain the upper hand over them. The king suspected that one of his own men was a spy working for the king of Israel (see 2 Kings 6:11). But one of the king's servants told him about Elisha the prophet, and how he could tell "12 the king of Israel the words that thou speakest in thy bedchamber" (2 Kings 6:12). So the king of Syria "sent [to Dothan where Elisha was] horses, and chariots, and a great host: and they came by night, and compassed the city about. And when the servant of the man of God was risen early, and gone forth, behold, an host compassed the city both with horses and chariots. And his servant said unto him, Alas, my master! how shall we do?" (2 Kings 6:14–15).

Let's just interrupt this story for a moment to reiterate that the concepts of the Vision of Faith, the Focus of Faith, and the Eye of Faith really have a lot of overlap. Stopping at this part of the story of Elisha, we could go back to the Vision of Faith, and discuss how Elisha's servant could only see the challenges and troubles in front of him, which prevented him from seeing the Lord's capacity to deliver them. We could also talk about it in terms of the Focus of Faith, and how the servant of Elisha needed to trust that the Lord would take care of His servants, no matter what experience they were about to endure. We could have discussed this story in those sections, but I really like how this story ties in with the Eye of Faith. There are a couple of things Elisha says that really stand out to me when he first calms the young man, and then pleads with the Lord to help the young man understand: "And he answered, Fear not: for they that *be* with us *are* more than they that *be* with them. And Elisha prayed, and said, Lord, I pray thee, open his eyes, that he may see. And the Lord opened the eyes of the young man; and he saw: and behold, the mountain *was* full of horses and chariots of fire round about Elisha" (2 Kings 6:16–17).

The first thing I notice is that Elisha tells him to "fear not." Maybe now is good time to remember that fear is in opposition to faith. That is why one will counter the other. So just as with the Vision of Faith where fear and doubt cloud our view of faith, we cannot see the power of God with the Eye of Faith when we fear. I understand that fear can be very difficult to overcome, if we talk about trying to "get rid of" fear. For purposes of the Vision of Faith and the Eye of Faith, all we really need to do is look past fear for long enough to see another possibility. It will take a lot of practice over a great many experiences to become "fearless." I think what is really expected from us is, despite our fear, to look unto God to catch a glimpse of something else. Then we nurture what we see.

The next thing I see here is that Elisha prayed that the young man's eyes would be opened that he might see. The result of this prayer is interesting to me. Notice that Elisha's prayer was answered, and the young man did have a change in perspective in that he saw that the mountain was full of horses and chariots. But I have to assume that seeing this vision did not change the young man's view of the Syrian army that originally alarmed him. I have to assume that he still saw the Syrians, and it was just that he no longer feared them, because he now also saw something more.

Elisha's prayer also helps us understand that the Lord's army was there before the young man saw it. All he saw was danger on every side when really there was help on every side even before the young man was aware of it. His eyes were opened with a change of perspective. When at first he felt that he was in the hands of his enemies (hence his cry "How shall we do!"), he was able to see that he was more in the hands of the Lord. We do not need to fear being the hands of our enemies when we are in the hands of our God.

The Eye of Faith does not in itself remove an obstacle. The Eye of Faith allows us to see past the obstacle to see the hand of the Lord. It is the Lord's hand that will eventually remove the obstacle (or maybe our hands through the help and power of the Lord). The Eye of Faith allows us to act in a way that is consistent with the obstacle being removed. The action on our part, consistent with what we see with the Eye of Faith is how the obstacle will be removed so that what we see with our natural eyes is the thing we saw previously with the Eye of Faith. However, just as in Elisha's story, there are things we cannot see with our mortal eyes. Some things we will only see with spiritual eyes. I submit that there will be some things in life that cannot be seen in our normal lives, but will only be possible to see with the Eye of Faith. Let me suggest that when you find yourself crying out "how shall I do?", first pray to see with a different perspective. Just like Elisha's servant, that different perspective will enable you to go forward in faith.

So now let's summarize what we understand about faith by again walking through the process of faith, applying what we now know about the specificity associated with the exercise of faith, and the principle of waiting on the Lord. Here's what I think I should do. When I encounter a circumstance that requires my faith, I step into the darkness of the unknown, knowing the power and goodness of God. When I step into the darkness, I place myself in the circumstance to be blessed by Him, as well as putting myself in a situation where I will need the blessings of the Lord to move forward. I do all I can to understand God's will, and act to align my thoughts and actions to His will. I try to envision an outcome in my mind, and I ask the Lord if the things I see are in line with His will. If I receive a positive confirmation, I pursue that vision with all my heart, acting in faith. If I do not receive a confirmation, I ask what the Lord would have me do. In essence, I ask to be given another clue to be able to see the Lord's will. Again, if I receive a confirmation, I follow it by acting accordingly. However, if I still do not feel that I have received a confirmation of the right path, I tell the Lord how I intend to live or how I intend to act, and then I pray and trust that He will bless me in it, and/or guide me to what I should be doing. I will continue on the path of faith, patiently waiting and relying on the Lord until I see the blessings of God open up in my life, no matter how long that takes. And when I grow weary and faint, I call out with all my heart for the Lord to bring me up again and renew my strength. I encourage each of us to follow a similar process so we can see with the Eye of Faith and even see with our eyes what we have seen with an Eye of Faith.

Note

1. Boyd K. Packer, "The Candle of the Lord," *Ensign*, January 1983.

HEART *of* FAITH

LET'S TALK FOR A MINUTE ABOUT COMPUTERIZED SECURITY systems. If you have ever seen any type of spy movie, or movie or television show where someone has a "secured" room, or any other similar thing, you have no doubt seen something about a computerized security system. Maybe the computerized system scans a fingerprint or handprint, or scans the retinas, or whatever else the system might do. Computerized security systems also exist in your real life, maybe with your computer or a password-protected phone, or a bank account or email account, or anything else where access is supposed to be restricted. Maybe they don't feel as fancy and don't have cool sounds and flashing lights, but a lot of the principles are still the same.

One of the similarities is that security systems can be bypassed or broken into if there isn't good security in place. With a weak security system, we will feel insecure about what we are trying to protect, whether it's a credit card number, or an email system, or something else. If we have reason to believe there is strong security in place, we feel a lot more comfortable that the thing we're trying to protect will stay protected. Some forms of security authorization rely on what is called "two-factor authentication" to try to increase the security. With two-factor authentication, the computer system requires two types of information before it will give you access, instead of just one. For example, when you use your bank ATM, it requires the use of an ATM card as well as a secret PIN. The card is something you have (one piece of the authentication), while the PIN is something you know (the other piece of the authentication). There are many other types.

Some two-factor authentication systems rely on a password or something like it, and some type of guarantee that you are who you say you are. Imagine that you put a secret spy room in your house and decided that your security system would require a password *and* a fingerprint scan. Such a security system could be said to provide security based on something that you *know* (the password), as well as something that you *are* (the fingerprint scan). That type of a security system would presumably be more secure (meaning, harder to deceive or harder to break into) than a security system based on either one alone.

Now let's talk about spiritual guidance. Someone who is trying to exercise faith or live the life expected of them by the Lord needs spiritual guidance. We discussed earlier that faith comes by the word of God and that we need to receive and accept it to exercise faith. We have commented that we need to seek the Lord's will to exercise the most powerful faith. Yet getting that spiritual guidance to identify the Lord's will can feel as challenging at times as exercising faith. But the Lord provides us with two-factor access to spiritual understanding that can help us receive true understanding so that we are not deceived. We can be secure in our exercise of faith because our spiritual understanding will be more secure. That two-factor access is based on receiving knowledge from the Holy Spirit. We should understand how we are to receive knowledge from the Spirit so that we can receive and follow the Lord's guidance.

Consider Doctrine and Covenants section 8: "Yea, behold, I will tell you in your mind and in your heart, by the Holy Ghost, which shall come upon you and which shall dwell in your heart. Now, behold, this is the spirit of revelation; behold, this is the spirit by which Moses brought the children of Israel through the Red Sea on dry ground" (D&C 8:2–3). Notice it says God will tell us in our minds *and* our hearts—both, not one or the other. God tells us things in our mind and heart together, which is more certain than what is just in our heart or what is just in our mind. When the Spirit guides us, we know it in our minds *and* we feel it in our hearts. The next phrase of the verse states that the Holy Ghost "shall come upon you *and* which shall dwell in your heart." We could read those in parallel to get the following understanding: I will tell you in your mind—by the Holy Ghost, which shall come upon you; and I will tell you in your heart—by the Holy Ghost, which shall dwell in your heart.

Spiritual guidance can come through two-factor access by something we know ("tell you in your mind"), in combination with something we feel or something that we are ("tell you . . . in your heart"). It frequently comes in that parallel form, where we perceive a flash of an idea or vision that lights up our minds, followed by the sustained glow of confirmation that lights up our hearts. We then say that we just "know" because we know it in our minds and feel we should follow it. By this, we can perceive that the thought or vision that came to our mind is true, because of the peace and comfort that stay with us as we contemplate and follow what came to us. When our mind and heart operate together, I believe our assurance of spiritual guidance is much stronger than if we try to look for only "inspired thoughts" or "feelings of truth." Rather, our heart can tell us that the thought we have is inspired, and the sense of peace and familiarity in our mind can tell us the thing we feel is inspired.

In my experience, we can receive spiritual guidance through our minds *and* our hearts in a couple of different ways. Sometimes our heart and mind light up at the same time, so we have a thought and at almost the same time we feel that what we are thinking is right. At other times, we receive a thought, and as we ponder that thought and consider carrying out action based on that thought, we feel that it is the right thing to do. Still other times, we will actually think on something and then begin to act on the thought before getting the accompanying feeling that we should continue to pursue it. In each circumstance, it is as though we feel we know the right thing to do, and as we contemplate that thing or when we start to act on it, we receive a confirming feeling in our hearts that it is indeed the right thing to do.

That feeling of confirmation can be a feeling of peace and calm about the thing. The feeling can be one of joy. I do not believe that Satan can imitate the feelings of peace or joy. Those feelings will only come from the Spirit of truth. Sometimes we start out thinking we know something is the right thing to do, and then hesitate. At that moment, the feeling of the Spirit can come in the form of a compelling feeling, compelling us to continue forward on the course we have started. In all of these cases, we exercise our faith by acting in accordance with our feeling, applying the Heart of Faith and trusting that God will come through for us. If we start to act and do not receive a confirming feeling, we can rightly question whether it is the guidance of the Spirit.

The Heart of Faith is a heart that is ready and willing to act on the things it feels are right, which confirm the truth in the mind. The Heart of Faith is a believing heart. Proverbs 3:5–6 tells us to "Trust in the Lord with all thine heart; and lean not unto thine own understanding. In all thy ways acknowledge him, and he shall direct thy paths." We have probably all seen examples of people with believing hearts who don't "lean to their own understanding." I don't take that phrase as a way out of engaging our own thoughts or applying our own effort. Instead I think of it as counsel to recognize the hand of the Lord above all. It reminds me that I should rely on the Lord rather than myself.

Enos, the son of Jacob in the Book of Mormon, had a believing heart. Let's review his story. Enos had a good father who taught him the things of the Lord (see Enos 1:1). Enos went hunting and ended up contemplating the words of his father (see Enos 1:3). Then we read the following: "And my soul hungered; and I kneeled down before my Maker, and I cried unto him in mighty prayer and supplication for mine own soul; and all the day long did I cry unto him; yea, and when the night came I did still raise my voice high that it reached the heavens. And there came a voice unto me, saying: Enos, thy sins are forgiven thee, and thou shalt be blessed. And I, Enos, knew that God could not lie; wherefore, my guilt was swept away. And I said: Lord, how is it done? And he said unto me: Because of thy faith in Christ, whom thou hast never before heard nor seen. And many years pass away before he shall manifest himself in the flesh; wherefore, go to, thy faith hath made thee whole" (Enos 1:4–8).

We see that by Enos's faith in Christ his sins were forgiven, and that his faith made him whole. What was Enos's faith?

How do you know that? Read that section over a couple of times until you can identify it. What does this story have to do with faith as we have been discussing it? How does that relate to the Heart of Faith?

I won't pretend to have all the answers, but I will tell you what I think this section shows about faith as we have been discussing it. Notice that when the voice came to Enos and said, "Thy sins are forgiven thee," Enos "knew that God could not lie; wherefore, [his] guilt was swept away." Enos trusted God, but not in some abstract sense—he knew that God could not lie (what he knew in his mind), and so he allowed his guilt to be completely removed (based on what he felt in his heart). God told him his sins were forgiven, and so he no longer felt any guilt—just like that. Importantly, see the effect on the Heart of Faith: it is willing to go wherever the Lord tells it to go, and it readily accepts what the Lord says.

Going back to our two-factor access to spiritual understanding, Enos knew the words of his father, who told him about "the joy of the saints" (verse 3), and he knew that God could not lie. He knew it, but it was when he felt it that he was certain it was true. Enos had the Heart of Faith that receives confirmation of the knowledge that lights up the mind. The Heart of Faith seeks out the Feeling of Faith. The Heart of Faith is not about doing whatever you "feel like." It is more about feeling what you are doing in faith. We could say that the Heart of Faith is the companion to the Eye of Faith. When what we see in our mind's eye is what we feel with the Heart of Faith, we see with our minds and we see with our hearts. In this way, we can be sure of the direction we should go, even if we do not completely understand the path. The Heart of Faith yearns for what we see with the Eye of Faith.

Notice one more thing about Enos's story in verse 7: "And I said: Lord, how is it done?" The first question Enos had when he felt the forgiveness that he sought was to wonder how it had been accomplished. I tend to think that my first reaction to such an experience would be to ask, "Really?" Or perhaps my reaction to the question is whether it can really be true. But Enos believed it was done and looked right past my initial reaction to the question of how it had been done. I have to think that Enos *felt* his guilt go away, and so he felt that it was done because he knew that God could not lie. The Heart of Faith has plenty of questions and asks plenty of questions, because it seeks to feel the truth. Because of what Enos felt with the Heart of Faith, he knew what had happened with him, and so he wanted to confirm that feeling in his soul by understanding the power behind it. That way when doubt may come up later in life, he would have something to fall back on. The Heart of Faith is etched with undeniable feelings of truth and light. So long as we do not deny our feelings but instead reflect on what we have experienced, the Heart of Faith will always keep us pointed in the right direction.

The Heart of Faith does not remain troubled when the Lord speaks peace to it, just as Enos allowed peace to come. In the remainder of the story of Enos, we see that Enos then desired the blessings that the Lord wanted to grant (see verses 9–17). His heart was in tune with God and the will of God. He allowed the peace of God to fill his soul. He then seemed to automatically desire the will of God. He knew that God had forgiven him, and he knew that God could bless the Nephites and the Lamanites. He felt desire for those blessings to come, and based on what he knew and what he felt, he aligned his will with God's. Verse 17 is very interesting, where Enos acknowledges: "And I, Enos, knew it would be according to the covenant which [God] had made; wherefore my soul did rest." And so our souls will rest as we allow our Heart of Faith to come in tune with the will of God.

TRIAL *of* FAITH

I really enjoyed my time living in the Pacific Northwest. One of the things I enjoyed with my family each year was taking advantage of all the Christmas tree farms where we could go and find a tree to take home and decorate at Christmastime. We'll ignore the irony of cutting down the Christmas symbol of everlasting life—and just focus on the great tradition and fun of selecting and decorating a Christmas tree each year. For any who have a similar personality as mine and my wife's, you know that when you go to select a tree you can look for a long time to find one that is "just right." Typically, you have a space in mind in the house that you are looking to fill up with just the right height and width for how you want to decorate your home. What that right one is can vary, but in general I think people are looking for trees with the right spacing of boughs and branches.

If you like Douglas firs, the ideal tree is full; the outer surface of the tree is as uniform as possible all the way around. If you like Nobles, the ideal tree has fairly uniform spacing of the boughs all the way around the tree. With either kind of tree, it can be very difficult to find one that is actually uniform, but instead they usually have at least one gaping hole that you will have to hide or cleverly decorate over. In the search for trees, my wife and I invariably find one we like that looks great from one side. However, examining the other side of the tree often reveals a big gap in the uniformity of the tree. My wife and I tended to place our tree in a corner somewhere in the house, and so we could tolerate a hole. It seemed that each year we found a tree we liked that would look great from "the front," and we would hide the hole in "the back." So, if you had come to our house at Christmastime to "inspect" our tree, you may very well have found a tree that looked ideal from one side, but not so much from the other side.

Recall how we learned with the Definition of Faith that the root of the words *faith* and *faithfulness* is also the root for the word *trustworthy*. We talked about how the path of faith is a two-way street. God is always faithful. We learn that we can always, always trust Him to do what He says. He will always come through. Because of this, we can exercise faith in God.

But what about us? Or to make it personal: What about me? Am I always faithful? Do I always come through? If you answer that question honestly, like me you will have answered, "No," or at least, "Not as much as I would like." Our faith relationship starts to look a lot like the Christmas trees I put in my house at Christmastime. From one side, the side of the Lord, it looks ideal. However, examination of the other side reveals gaps or holes in my faithfulness. The fact is that I have work to do to be as trustworthy as the Lord is with me.

And that is where the Trial of Faith comes in. We will not have a chance to prove greater faithfulness without putting our faith to the test. As bitter as it sounds, we have to experience the Trial of Faith for our faith to be strengthened. We have to climb uphill to reach the top of a mountain or overcome the mountain, and we have to work out our faith to build spiritual strength.

There are several stories that illustrate different points related to the Trial of Faith. We'll only deal with a select few here. First, we'll see that the Trial of Faith can open the path that God wants us to take. Were it not for the trial, we may not find that path to take us where He wants us to go. Next, we'll see that the Trial of Faith proves us, and gives us an opportunity to prove the Lord. Last, we'll see that the Trial of Faith can test the very core of what we believe to give us wholehearted, unshaken faith in the Lord. So, let's get right into it.

Our Trials Open God's Path for Us

In Exodus 14, we read of the great exodus of the nation of Israel from Egypt under the direction of Moses. Recall that after the plagues came, Pharaoh was finally persuaded to allow the nation of Israel to leave. Not too long after that, no doubt realizing just how much work their slaves had been doing for them, he said, "Why have we done this, that we have let Israel go from serving us? And he made ready his chariot, and took his people with him" (Exodus 14:5–6).

So, Pharaoh and his army catch up to Israel in the wilderness, "And when Pharaoh drew nigh, the children of Israel lifted up their eyes, and, behold, the Egyptians marched after them; and they were sore afraid: and the children of Israel cried out unto the Lord. And they said unto Moses, Because there were no graves in Egypt, hast thou taken us away to die in the wilderness? wherefore hast thou dealt thus with us, to carry us forth out of Egypt? Is not this the word that we did tell thee in Egypt, saying, Let us alone, that we may serve the Egyptians? For it had been better for us to serve the Egyptians, than that we should die in the wilderness" (Exodus 14:10–12). Before we get too disappointed with Israel losing hope so quickly, let's stop and think about what these verses reveal for a moment. They had been in bondage for *generations*—these people and generations before them had known nothing but life in Egypt. They certainly feared the Egyptians, or they probably would have tried to rise up and leave sooner. This people probably had already struggled in starting their journey, uprooting families and now living on the move.

Imagine what they struggled with here: the Lord had promised to deliver them, and they took a huge chance, putting their very lives and the lives of their families on the line to trust that He actually would. Now here they were out in unfamiliar territory in the middle of the wilderness and it sure looked like they were about to die there. They complain to Moses, and ask: What are we doing here? Were there not enough gravesites in Egypt to be buried there, so you had to bring us out here to be slaughtered? And then their budding faith began to weaken as they decided it would have "been better for us to serve the Egyptians, than that we should die in the wilderness."

Don't we frequently do the same thing? The Lord promises to deliver us, or help us, or He answers our prayers, and then we turn around and lose faith as soon as the next Trial of Faith hits us. After the plagues, Israel may have thought leaving Egypt would be the easy part. They probably thought deliverance was provided in leaving Egypt. Who knew that they were just starting off with the challenges? Would they have agreed to come if they knew what they were going to have to experience once they left Egypt? There are probably some who would have. I know with me personally there are certainly times I think that since the Lord came through for me once, things should go smoothly after that. As we continue with the story of Moses leading Israel, we learn that things frequently don't go smoothly.

Moses tries to buoy their faith. He identifies two things that I know I need to remember in situations where I start to lose my faith. "And Moses said unto the people, Fear ye not, stand still, and see the salvation of the Lord, which he will shew to you to day: for the Egyptians whom ye have seen to day, ye shall see them again no more for ever. The Lord shall fight for you, and ye shall hold your peace" (Exodus 14:13–14). The first thing he says is "Fear ye not." When we fear, we cannot trust. Fear will keep you from doing your part, and so it has the effect of both preventing you from doing your part, as well as losing trust that the Lord will come through with His. Fear causes us to question the Lord's faithfulness, and it causes us to lose our faithfulness. It attacks both sides of the two-way street of faith.

The second thing Moses says is "stand still." In my mind, this admonition means I shouldn't lose my head. I need to calm down and not make too big a deal out of everything. In essence, he tells them not to panic. Panic is that feeling we experience when it seems everything is outside of our control, and we think we should be able to, or be allowed to, control it. However, giving up control of our circumstances does not need to result in panic, if we give up control to the Lord. When we give up control, we cannot just give up. We shouldn't stop trying to do the things we are capable of. But we need to recognize that there are a lot of things we ultimately cannot control, and we need to learn to let the Lord use those things to shape us and guide us.

Moses gives the promise that if we will keep our fear in check (fear not), and if we keep our heads cool to continue doing what the Lord has sent us to do (stand still), "The Lord shall fight for [us], and [we] shall hold our peace." We will allow the Lord to open our path, and we should not question or complain when the Lord asks something of us. Since it is His path, He will fight for us. When Israel reaches the shore of the Red Sea, we see this point illustrated.

However, before we get there, we can learn something else from this story. There is an apparent gap in the account in Exodus. In verses 13 and 14, we read of Moses encouraging the children of Israel (quoted above). And then in the immediately following verses we read: "And the Lord said unto Moses, Wherefore criest thou unto me? speak unto the children of Israel, that they go forward: But lift thou up thy rod, and stretch out thine hand over the sea, and divide it: and the children of Israel shall go on dry ground through the midst of the sea" (Exodus 14:15–16).

We do not have direct record of Moses crying unto the Lord about all of this, but we learn indirectly here that Moses took all this to the Lord. That's what we're supposed to do, right? But let me ask if you, like me, have ever found yourself in the following situation. I feel that the Lord has directed me to do something. As I think about what the Lord wants me to do, I realize that it is going to be hard. In fact, it seems like it is going to be very hard or maybe feels nearly impossible, and I start to not want to do it. Have you ever felt like that? Have you then done as I have done, and decided that before going out and doing like you are supposed to do, you will just sit on it for a while, and maybe pray about it some more, and ask the Lord to help you to do it? And then after waiting some time to get started, you start to pray harder for the Lord to help you with it, or maybe pray harder for the Lord to help you get started, and you think some more about how hard it will be to do it, which makes you feel like waiting a little longer to get started, which makes you feel like praying more for help to do it. I used a run-on sentence on purpose here: I can cycle like that over and over and spend *a lot* of time inactive when I should be up and doing.

The Lord makes clear that He just wants Moses to *do* what he has been instructed to do. We can assume from the Lord's answer that the Lord already promised the help Moses would need. The Lord already gave the command for Moses and the children of Israel to get started. God didn't need Moses to petition Him some more to be convinced to help them. When He asks us to do something, likewise, we don't need so much to petition Him to show us the path and guide us, as we need to show courage to do what we know we should and ask for the Lord to bless our efforts. The Lord's side of the "Christmas tree" is in good shape, and we need to start working on our side.

Now, I believe that God is very patient with us in these circumstances. He understands our fear and our hesitation. Notice that His rebuke to Moses, while direct, is not harsh. He asks Moses, "Wherefore criest thou unto me?" which we might rephrase as "What are you doing coming again to ask for help in what I already told you I would help?" He then commands, "Speak unto the children of Israel, that they go forward." He wants them to get up and just start to do what He asked. That is the simple yet difficult secret to obeying in so many of life's circumstances—we just need to start.

And so Moses gets the people to start to act on the word of the Lord they had received. Our account continues: "And Moses stretched out his hand over the sea; and the Lord caused the sea to go back by a strong east wind all that night, and made the sea dry land, and the waters were divided. And the children of Israel went into the midst of the sea upon the dry ground: and the waters were a wall unto them on their right hand, and on their left" (Exodus 14:21–22). Notice that it says that "the Lord caused the sea to go back by a strong east wind all that night, and made the sea dry land, and the waters were divided," but it doesn't say how long it took for them to divide. I typically imagine that the waters parted immediately, but we don't know that, which leads me to a couple of different thoughts.

With the size of the exodus here, it probably would have taken all night for all the children of Israel to cross the Red Sea, so maybe that is all that is meant by the strong east wind blowing all that night—it blew all night to give everyone the chance to cross. Even assuming that the parting occurred immediately, we have to assume that some of the people were sitting in the back waiting for their turn to cross. They may have been sitting for hours, with the threat of the Egyptians coming along at any time. Let's also remember that the people are out in the wilderness. Have you been camping or hiking out in a deserted place and felt the wind come on? The word that comes to my mind is *dust*. The area out near the Red Sea is a lot of desert, so maybe *dust* should be understood as *sandstorm*. So, on top of the concern that the Egyptians could be upon them at any time, there is the other fact that a "strong" wind blew "all that night," which makes me think at least part of the group got blasted with dust and sand for hours. I must admit that if I were one of the children of Israel waiting on the banks of the Red Sea with Pharaoh's army held off by a cloud (see Exodus 14:19–20), this dust storm would hardly feel like the deliverance I was hoping for.

Then there is the possibility that maybe the waters didn't part immediately for anyone, and all of them had to sit and be blasted by wind and sand for a period of time before their path through the Red Sea opened up to them. In that case, the expected deliverance could have actually seemed like a disappointment. Imagine Moses "stretched out his hand over the sea," and then what happened? The wind started blowing. In that case, I imagine Moses putting his arms down and then stretching them out again, and again the only effect is wind. Maybe he shakes his staff at the water a bit, but all he gets is wind. Some of my deliverances have sure felt like that, and it is only in hindsight that I realize that what seemed like another trial was actually the promised deliverance.

Let's understand a very important point about deliverance from this story: the Lord's deliverance was hugely dramatic, but it happened over a period of time, and for all we know it could have seemed anticlimactic. And herein we find the real Trial of Faith. Let's recall Moses's words to "fear not" and "stand still" to see the salvation of the Lord. A strong wind blowing dust through your camp all night might feel like another trial instead of the deliverance you were hoping for. And yet it is in this very thing that the hand of God was shown. For that wind blew all night long "and made the sea dry land, and the waters were divided." This is what I want to take away from this story: the deliverance of the Lord will often come in a form we are not expecting. There are many times that we think we've already endured the Trial of Faith only to be hit with another round of difficulty, and then maybe another; and it is only after the last round of difficulty that we see the Lord has opened the way to the path we are supposed to go. And then we still need to take it. The trial of wind made the dry land appear, and the people had to find the faith to walk out into the sea on that dry land. The trial of wind probably made that night feel very long. The children of Israel had to endure that trial all night long before their hoped-for deliverance was manifested.

It was only after they had passed through the waters, taking the path the Lord had commanded with walls of water on either side, when the children of Israel saw the truly dramatic evidence of God's deliverance they had been waiting for. I will let you read Exodus 14:23–31 to recall the account of how the Egyptians pursued the children of Israel, and the Lord commanded Moses to stretch his hands again over the waters to watch the "sea returned to his strength." That account provides the witness of Moses's words, but that witness was a long, tough night off from when the promise was made.

Like the children of Israel, there are times we will feel desperate for deliverance and we don't know how or when the Lord will deliver us. But just like He did for the children of Israel, He will protect us while His plan goes into motion, just as with the angel and the cloud that held off the Egyptians during the trial of wind. We may be asked to endure another trial when we expect deliverance, because it will open the path to where the Lord wants us to go. It is usually only after walking the path that the Lord has opened for us that we can look back and see the dramatic deliverance the Lord prepared for us, and that He guided us along. The keys to enduring the Trial of Faith are to "fear not" and "stand still." And as we saw, "stand still" can actually mean for us to get up and get going but with stillness in our hearts and minds.

How we endure trials tells us a lot about the maturity of our faith. The story of Israel shows a people young in their faith, who complained when things became difficult. I imagine they could not perceive, in their trial, that the trials themselves were actually the best path for them to get where they wanted to get. Let me share a personal experience where I learned that the road to where I wanted to go in life can sometimes lead through the Trial of Faith.

My wife and I had purchased our first home and were excited to stay there a long time. But after living there for a couple of years and finding out the house wasn't all we had hoped it was, the company I worked for moved a couple of cities away, and we started to talk about moving. We had a strong feeling about selling our home and moving closer to work, so we acted on our impressions. What followed was a series of unfortunate events with results that played out over the course of several years. Our challenges started as the housing market crashed the month after we purchased our more expensive new home; then I had a reversal of fortunes at work that resulted in significantly less pay; and then I was involved in a car accident that totaled my car and left me needing physical and emotional recovery. While all this played out, we added two children to our family and became overwhelmed with the effort required to deal with some chronic family health issues.

We were unable to keep that house, and could no longer afford to own a home, so we became renters. We were praying constantly for the Lord to help us and guide us to where we needed to go. Much of the time it didn't feel like there was anyone there listening. You could even say we were a little like the children of Israel on their exodus: we were excited to go to the promised land as we left our first home, until we found ourselves in the desert questioning whether it might have just been better to stay. We eventually decided we had to leave behind our neighborhood and our friends to move across town to a little house with lower rent. This was our fourth move in four years.

I think the promised land came later for my family, as we still had several years of difficulty ahead of us at that point, and even as I write this I wouldn't quite say we're in the promised land we thought we were headed to when we left that first home. While we aren't there yet, in hindsight we can see that those trials started us on the path to the promised land and we just didn't understand what the journey was going to look like. The children of Israel started their path towards the promised land when they crossed the Red Sea, although they still had years of traveling through the wilderness before they arrived.

I wish I could say that I didn't complain when the Lord did not come through in the way I wanted Him to throughout my family's trials, but I can't. We have honestly made every effort to do what we thought we should, although the journey has been difficult. There were several times we thought we had faced the trial that would then lead us to where we wanted to be. But we weren't there yet.

I have learned many things from these experiences. First, I need to work on patiently waiting for the Lord to come through. Hopefully the Lord has seen that I am willing to follow impressions and will know He can trust me to follow them, no matter what the outcome of those impressions is. Another thing I am reminded of over and over again is that the exercise of faith requires us to keep our focus, as discussed in the sections above. There are times I shifted focus from trusting the Lord to use His wisdom in dealing with me as He sees fit, to wondering why I couldn't just get on with *my* life plans. I am learning that we have to be willing to wait on the Lord even when we want to race ahead with our own plans. As I look back, I understand that a great number of blessings have come to me and my family as we have taken a path we didn't realize we were on. One other thing I have learned is that sometimes the Lord will ask us to do things to test our patience and to test our faith, to see if we will obey without complaint. And that leads us into our next story.

The Lord Tries Our Patience and Our Faith

In Mosiah 23, we read of the people of Alma escaping from a wicked ruler, King Noah. They were blessed right from the beginning, with the Lord warning Alma that the king was sending his armies to destroy them and the Lord strengthening the people to be able to escape (see Mosiah 23:1–2). They were further blessed to find a great place to live (see verses 4–5). The people lived in peace, their new leaders taught them to live righteously, and they prospered in the things the Lord had blessed them with (see verses 15 and 19). This is all going so well—a people delivered and blessed by the hand of Lord. Let's put "And they all lived happily ever after" on this story and call it good.

Instead, we read: "Nevertheless the Lord seeth fit to chasten his people; yea, he trieth their patience and their faith" (Mosiah 23:21). That sounds foreboding. Remember, this is the same Lord that just delivered and blessed them. Why would He now "try their patience and their faith"? We'll look at this story a couple of times to try to understand this process of patience and faith. For now, let's just go on to read about their Trial of Faith and what they experienced.

We learn from verses 30–35 that an army of Lamanites becomes lost and stumbles upon Alma and his people. Alma and his people surrender themselves to the Lamanite army, trusting that God will again deliver them (see verses 25–29). The Lamanite army takes possession of the lands of the people of Alma, sets guards around their land, and allows a man named Amulon to rule over them (see verses 36–39).

Now the real Trial of Faith began. In Mosiah 24:8, we read: "Amulon began to exercise authority over Alma and his brethren, and began to persecute him, and cause that his children should persecute their children." The next verses continue by explaining that Amulon "put tasks upon them, and put task-masters over them. And it came to pass that so great were their afflictions that they began to cry mightily to God" (Mosiah 24:9–10). Just consider this for a moment. We have a people (Alma and his brethren) who are trying to live in peace, just doing what they're supposed to be doing. They were not accused by man or God of doing anything wrong or making any mistakes. So these trials do not appear to have anything to do with chastisement for wrongdoing. They were simply required to go through a rough patch of life. They were in the wrong place at the wrong time and ended up with a set of difficult circumstances through no choice or fault of their own and despite being righteous and seeking after God.

The people of Israel that we discussed above were required to endure a Trial of Faith as part of the deliverance process. They struggled and complained during that trial. The people of Alma had already been delivered, and were then allowed to land in bad circumstances. Sometimes bad things will happen to us in life. Furthermore, the response of the people of Alma was exactly what I strive for in my life: when faced with trial, "they began to cry mightily to God." What a faithful people! They didn't even complain! They just prayed for help. They had learned to rely on prayer, just as they had relied on God to deliver them.

But instead of getting better, things got worse: "And Amulon commanded them that they should stop their cries; and he put guards over them to watch them, that whosoever should be found calling upon God should be put to death" (Mosiah 24:11). Where was God's help and blessing to this people that had sought to do what was right? Prayer was now a crime subject to capital punishment. The one thing they were *sure* would help them was now not an option to them, or at least not in a formal prayer sort of way. So they turned to the only thing they felt they had left, and prayed in their hearts: "And Alma and his people did not raise their voices to the Lord their God, but did pour out their hearts to him; and he did know the thoughts of their hearts" (Mosiah 24:12).

I have had personal experience with feeling "unable" to pray in my trials, although my trouble has nothing to do with threats as with the people of Alma. But there are times I just feel cut off from prayer, especially in my trials. I just cannot seem to pray. I don't seem to have a problem praying when things are going well, but I will struggle with it when I need the help the most. Sometimes I don't feel capable of approaching the Lord in prayer, in the strict sense of kneeling and uttering a prayer. In those times, these verses have helped me. Even when I cannot feel to raise my voice to God, I can and do pour out my heart to Him as I am going about my day. I pray in my heart that I can be brought to be humble enough to pray, and this usually helps. Even though prayer is probably preferred, I believe the Lord will hear and know the thoughts of our hearts when we struggle, even if we feel like we are prevented from prayer as though some invisible guard is threatening us for the act.

Now back to the people of Alma—on top of falling into bad circumstances, the deliverance that the people of Alma had come to expect in normal circumstances was not available to them. The story never says the people had any problem with praying or with being sincere in their prayers, as I have experienced in my life. But I have to suspect that these circumstances brought them to fully turn their every thought and feeling to the Lord. We will learn to do the same in those trials where our normal strengths fail us. Those are hard trials when we get to the point where nothing familiar seems to produce a result.

But we cannot give up hope. As you turn your whole heart, your whole soul, and every thought to God, you will also feel the comfort that His Spirit can bring. With the people of Alma, we read "And it came to pass that the voice of the Lord came to them in their afflictions, saying: Lift up your heads and be of good comfort, for I know of the covenant which ye have made unto me; and I will covenant with my people and deliver them out of bondage." The Lord promised them that He would deliver them. He did not say when.

As I write this, I recall two separate prayers about two separate challenges in my life that I made—one about four years ago, and the other about six years ago. I felt God's Spirit as I prayed, and I felt His voice assuring me that He would deliver me. But as I write this, I am still waiting for deliverance on both of them. I am still waiting for the results of the Lord's assurances. I don't tell you this to discourage you. We need to remember that the Lord is wiser than we could ever understand in this life. I tell you to encourage you. Oh, the things I have experienced and learned in the last four and six years under these challenges! And after all this time I have seen that subsequent challenges don't tend to rattle me as much. It now takes stronger trials to rattle me! And those have come as well.

When you experience trials, internalize the comfort that the Lord offers the people of Alma. He says: "I will also ease the burdens which are put upon your shoulders, that even you cannot feel them upon your backs, even while you are in bondage; and this will I do that ye may stand as witnesses for me hereafter, and that ye may know of a surety that I, the Lord God, do visit my people in their afflictions" (Mosiah 24:14). Christ did not say that He would come to His children immediately and relieve them of everything they were struggling with, but He did promise to lighten their burdens "in their afflictions." That is a comforting thought. Our God is an all-weather God. We know that He is there in fair weather and that He blesses us with our righteous desires according to His will and pleasure. In this example, I believe that God is demonstrating that He is also with us in the storms of life and that He will bless us to be able to endure them well. We don't know exactly how long Alma and his people were in bondage, but we are told that "it came to pass that the burdens which were laid upon Alma and his brethren were made light; yea, the Lord did strengthen them that they could bear up their burdens with ease, and they did submit cheerfully and with patience to all the will of the Lord" (Mosiah 24:15).

We read that "the Lord did strengthen them" so that they not only endured their burdens but "they could bear up their burdens with ease." Importantly, we learn of the faithfulness of the people that "they did *cheerfully* and *with patience*" submit to "all the will of the Lord." I'm still trying to learn to be cheerful and patient after years of experiencing challenges. While I am still working on it, I believe my cheer will come from holding fast to the assurance that the Lord gave me years ago that He would deliver me. I haven't seen it yet, and there have been times that I have started to doubt it would ever come. But I have felt the peace of the Lord since, and now the longer I go without being delivered, the surer I am that His deliverance will come, even though I do not know how or when. It helps me be more patient. I can just go about doing what I know I am supposed to do and what I am required to do, and wait for the Lord to fulfill His promises in His way and in His time.

Remember that the people of Alma had faith that was already proven through dealing with trials. Their new circumstances became another Trial of Faith that tested the faith they already had. Like them, efforts we have made in response to past challenges will not always provide us with relief or deliverance as quickly as we might expect based on previous experience. In contrast to the proven faith of the people of Alma, the people of Israel were learning how to apply new faith. The faith of the people of Israel grew and developed as they saw that their trials led them down the path the Lord wanted them to take. The faith of the people of Alma was strengthened as they learned to wait on the Lord. He gave assurance here and there that He was still aware of their circumstances. And then He allowed them to learn to live, day after day, following after what they were sure was right even when the Lord's hand did not manifest itself in the way they hoped.

But in the end, the Lord always rewards His faithful, and the Trial of Faith comes to an end. And so it was with the people of Alma. "And it came to pass that so great was their faith and their patience that the voice of the Lord came unto them again, saying: Be of good comfort, for on the morrow I will deliver you out of bondage. And he said unto Alma: Thou shalt go before this people, and I will go with thee and deliver this people out of bondage. Now it came to pass that Alma and his people in the night-time gathered their flocks together, and also of their grain; yea, even all the night-time were they gathering their flocks together. And in the morning the Lord caused a deep sleep to come upon the Lamanites, yea, and all their task-masters were in a profound sleep. And Alma and his people departed into the wilderness" (Mosiah 24:16–20).

We are never provided a direct explanation of why the people suffered this trial, or what came of the Lord trying their patience and their faith. As I read the scriptures we have, they do not reveal a higher purpose in the mind of the Lord. We may not understand in this life why we were made to experience the trials we do, or understanding how and when they simply "disappear." Our deliverance might be the parting of a sea or the sleeping of our captors. In any circumstance, our testimony will be that God strengthens us in trial and delivers us from affliction.

When we understand that, we will better understand why the people of Alma "poured out their thanks to God because he had been merciful unto them, and eased their burdens, and had delivered them out of bondage; for they were in bondage, and none could deliver them except it were the Lord their God" (Mosiah 24:21). Notice that when they were in bondage, or when they were experiencing their Trial of Faith, they eventually did "pour out their hearts to [God]" (verse 12), which helped them through the trial. When the trial was over, they "poured out their thanks to God" (verse 21). I would suggest that their trials changed them, and as they learned to pour out their hearts to God, it became a part of how they lived. So even when their deliverance must have taken much longer than they hoped, they didn't complain that it took so long—instead they poured out their hearts in thanks that it had come. I think that true gratitude is not just a swelling of emotion in seeing our faith or patience or effort being rewarded; true gratitude is an awareness that you wouldn't trade your current experience for an easier opportunity. It is awareness that your experience has changed you, and that your challenges have become a part of who you are.

Now that we have seen how they dealt with their Trial of Faith and how the Lord did eventually deliver them, let's go back to a part we skipped in Mosiah 23: "Nevertheless—whosoever putteth his trust in him the same shall be lifted up at the last day. Yea, and thus it was with this people. For behold, I will show unto you that they were brought into bondage, and none could deliver them but the Lord their God, yea, even the God of Abraham and Isaac and of Jacob. And it came to pass that he did deliver them, and he did show forth his mighty power unto them, and great were their rejoicings" (Mosiah 23:22–24). We just saw their great rejoicings. We saw that they were in bondage and that God did deliver them out of it. I think we learn that God's "mighty power" is sometimes very quiet. But there is something I found interesting as I read through this story again.

Verse 22 says that "whosoever putteth his trust in [God] the same shall be *lifted up at the last day*" (emphasis added). I had always taken that to mean that people would be blessed in Heaven when their life on Earth ended. But if we continue in verse 23, it says, "and thus it was with this people." The people of Alma were delivered—they didn't die. So what does it mean that he who trusts will be "lifted up at the last day"? Even if it ultimately means blessed at Judgment Day (which I believe is true), maybe it also has to do with something in *this life* that "this people" experienced.

Let's consider for a moment that the "last day" refers to the last day of our Trial of Faith. That last day of trial could be the end of our mortal lives, but it could also mean the last day of a specific trial experienced in life. With this thought in mind, I want to take you to a verse I have read many times before but had never thought anything of it. In Alma 47:22–23, we read, "But behold, as the king came out to meet him Amalickiah caused that one of his servants should go forth to meet the king. And they went and bowed themselves before the king, as if to reverence him because of his greatness. And it came to pass that the king put forth his hand to raise them, as was the custom with the Lamanites, as a token of peace, which custom they had taken from the Nephites."

Notice that the custom of the people was to bow before the king, who would then raise them up (or maybe we could say *lift them up*?). It was their duty to reverence the king, and they bowed until "it came to pass that the king put forth his hand to raise them." Just as it was their duty to bow to reverence the king, presumably it was up to the pleasure of the king to address them when he felt like it. Thus, I imagine they would stay bowed for a long time if he did not feel ready to address them. Presumably the king could leave them there for minutes or even hours if it suited him, and they would be expected to remain there until "the king put forth his hand to raise them." An earthly king may require us to wait for as long as *he wants*, for whatever arbitrary reason he wants us to wait. But our Heavenly King will have us stay bowed, doing our duty, for as long *we need* to learn what we need to learn from the trial. When the Lord feels we have learned and grown to where we need to be, He will put forth His hand and deliver us from the trial. Now let's apply this to the story we were reading. Remember, our verse says that "whosoever putteth his trust in [God] . . . shall be lifted up at the last day." When do we need lifting up? I think the obvious answer is when we are down. The Trial of Faith and the circumstances of life can cause us to bow down under a heavy burden—life can beat us down. And when we're down and we pray to God and He promises to deliver us, we need to remember our duty. It is our duty to remain where we are, carrying on faithful in our duty until it comes to pass that He lifts us up. It is up to the pleasure of our Heavenly King when to put forth His hand to raise us. We show our trust and reverence to God and His wisdom by learning to wait on the Lord and enduring the Trial of Faith.

We cannot tell what lessons God has in store for us. What we should do is submit ourselves to the will of the Lord and wait upon the Lord until He sees fit to raise us up. And when

He does, it is the last day of the trial. The Lamanite king would raise his servants as a token of peace. Our Heavenly King will lift us up and fill us with peace. We just need to keep trusting and doing our duty until He does, even we are required to wait on the Lord for some indeterminate period of time as the people of Alma.

Now let's talk again about the promise that Moroni gives regarding the Trial of Faith. He says in Ether 12:6, "And now, I, Moroni, would speak somewhat concerning these things; I would show unto the world that faith is things which are hoped for and not seen; wherefore, dispute not because ye see not, for ye receive no witness until after the trial of your faith." If faith is a two-way street, we can think of the Trial of Faith as a two-way street as well. On the one hand, the Trial of Faith puts us in a circumstance where we prove ourselves faithful to God, whatever difficulty comes our way. On the other hand, the Trial of Faith gives us an opportunity to prove that God is faithful in every circumstance. We may have to completely change our perspective, or fight against a number of fears or habits we have. But when we can hold on to what we have felt, what a powerful witness we will receive of the faithfulness of God!

Notice that I said we need to hold onto what we have felt, rather than what we feel. There have been a number of times in trial that I get completely absorbed in the difficulty I am having, so all I feel is struggle, or perhaps I feel abandoned. Typically, when I start to recognize a trial, I start to pray for help. At some point, I will feel peace about that trial and will feel an assurance of deliverance. I then need to hold onto what I *felt* and not get distracted by what I *feel* as the trial and difficulties continue. When I remember what I felt, it can help me hold on a little longer, as long as I am willing to put a little more of my heart into what I felt. It is an anchor to my faith (see Ether 12:4). When I remember what I felt, it can help me again feel peace and feel assurance that the Lord will deliver me, even if I must wait on His deliverance.

What do we experience when we hold on in faith? We see the Lord guiding us through our trials. We see the Lord preparing us to receive blessings that we otherwise could not receive. We see the Lord making us ready to understand and serve our fellow man. We eventually see the purpose to our faith. But we won't necessarily see the reason behind our trials. We don't need to know specifically why the Lord allows us to pass through trial to be able to witness that as we turn to the Lord, His hand guides and blesses us. At first the people of Alma did not see. They waited on the Lord in hope of receiving deliverance. Once delivered by God in His way, the people believed that "none could deliver them except it were the Lord their God" (Mosiah 24:21). They allowed the Lord to provide the kind of deliverance He wanted to and did not put requirements on the Lord for the kind of help they wanted. Thus, they bore their burdens with patience, and they saw deliverance by simply pressing forward doing the work that was put upon them in their trial. They did not dispute with the Lord or complain to Him that they shouldn't have to pass through such a difficult trial.

Rather, they did what was required because they knew the Lord would guide them. Wherefore, they did not dispute, and they received a witness that God knows where to lead us, and how to teach us through the Trial of Faith. Like them, we need to learn to "dispute not" with the wisdom of the Lord in allowing the Trial of Faith to come upon us. As we learn to stop asking "why me" and simply start keeping our part of being faithful, we will feel the assurance that the Lord will be with us in our trial, and He will eventually deliver us. Like our Christmas tree, we'll be more focused on admiring the Lord's ideal faithfulness (the ideal part on display) and fixing our own faithfulness (the part hidden in the corner), instead of looking for flaws in the tree.

The Trial of Faith provides us an opportunity to build upon the Rock of Christ. Paul spoke of building upon the foundation of Jesus Christ in 1 Corinthians 3:10–14, "But let every man take heed how he buildeth thereupon. For other foundation can no man lay than that is laid, which is Jesus Christ. Now if any man build upon this foundation gold, silver, precious stones, wood, hay, stubble; Every man's work shall be made manifest: for the day shall declare it, because it shall be revealed by fire; and the fire shall try every man's work of what sort it is. If any man's work abide which he hath built thereupon, he shall receive a reward." We build our faith upon the foundation of Jesus Christ. We need to take heed how we build on that foundation, because "the fire shall try every man's work" to find out what we are made of or "of what sort" we are.

The first thing I take from Paul's words is that we will be tried. We are commanded to have faith in God to receive the blessings we want from life. The only known way to test for those blessings is for the "fire" or the Trial of Faith to "try every man's work." Notice how we have now come back to the word "try." Let's go back to the beginning of the story of the people of Alma and recall that the story starts off by saying that the Lord "trieth their patience and their faith" (Mosiah 23:21). Now let's go all the way back to the section the Definition of Faith and recall that when we read Hebrews 11 in Portuguese, we came across the verb *provar*, meaning "to *prove*" as through a *trial* or test, and Alma 32:33 where we read that we will know the seed is good as it swells and sprouts because we have "*tried* the experiment." Suddenly we start to see things coming full-circle. We try the word to see that the

Lord is always faithful. The Lord tries us to teach us to always be faithful and not doubt. And so faith and the Trial of Faith are two-way streets. It seems for me that when the Lord tries me, He reveals where the gaps are in my Christmas tree of faith that I have tried to hide in the corner. Instead of hiding in a corner, I need to stand up to the Trial of Faith, find the path the Lord wants me to get on, and wait on the Lord to gain the strength to perfect that faith.

Peter provided some similar thoughts to Paul, and actually used the phrase that became the title to this section. In 1 Peter 1, he teaches: "Blessed be the God and Father of our Lord Jesus Christ, which according to his abundant mercy hath begotten us again unto a lively hope by the resurrection of Jesus Christ from the dead, To an inheritance incorruptible, and undefiled, and that fadeth not away, reserved in heaven for you, Who are kept by the power of God through faith unto salvation ready to be revealed in the last time. Wherein ye greatly rejoice, though now for a season, if need be, ye are in heaviness through manifold temptations: That the trial of your faith, being much more precious than of gold that perisheth, though it be tried with fire, might be found unto praise and honour and glory at the appearing of Jesus Christ: Whom having not seen, ye love; in whom, though now ye see him not, yet believing, ye rejoice with joy unspeakable and full of glory: Receiving the end of your faith, even the salvation of your souls" (1 Peter 1:3–9).

Peter introduces a hope in the resurrection to be raised up to salvation in Heaven. God keeps us by His power, *through faith*. We greatly rejoice in the hope of this salvation, "though now for a season . . . [we] are in heaviness through manifold temptations." So, we look forward to a great reward even though we feel the heaviness of trials now. And then Peter talks about the Trial of Faith. Specifically, he says that our faith is more precious than gold or earthly treasures that perish or are gone when we leave this life. Our faith may be "tried with fire." Here both Paul and Peter agree that we will be tried with fire. So, what is that fire?

Malachi 3:2 makes reference to Jesus Christ being like a "refiner's fire." Paul and Peter refer to the treasures of the earth which are refined with fire to get to their purified state in which their true beauty is revealed. Through the Trial of Faith, our refiner, Jesus Christ, refines us to a more purified state where our true beauty is revealed. Then we "might be found unto praise and honour and glory at the appearing of Jesus Christ."

And Peter finishes with a declaration of faith that summarizes what we have talked about. He says that though we have not yet seen Jesus Christ, we love Him; and though we do not yet see Him, we believe and work toward receiving the end of our faith. Again, faith is hope in that which we have not yet seen, but it is the assurance we feel that causes us to believe and work toward the end or object of our faith. We trust that we will receive what God has promised, and we act on that trust. Our Refiner is also the Author and Finisher of our faith.

But just as with the refinement of a precious stone or precious metal, there is usually a process of heating to obtain the final purified product. The refiner's application of heat to the raw material represents a trial of the raw material as it gets refined. In our lives, we need to endure the Trials of Faith to overcome every doubt, as our Refiner purifies us. Some of those doubts can cut very deep and make it challenging for us to go on. When we find the strength to carry on despite the doubt and the challenge, our faith will be strong like those whose names are synonymous with faithfulness, which brings us to the story of Abraham.

Through Trials We Overcome Every Doubt

Before introducing Abraham's story, I want to talk about Star Wars, which started out as a trilogy of movies by George Lucas, and which has grown into an enterprise now owned by Disney. In the movie *Return of the Jedi*, Luke has a conversation with his Jedi Master, Yoda, about completing his training to become a Jedi Knight so he can be ready to defeat Darth Vader. During the conversation, Yoda tells Luke that he does not need any more training, and Luke then decides with amazement that he is already a Jedi. Yoda tells him that he is not quite a Jedi, but first he must face Vader. Luke fears Vader and fears what will happen if he faces him again, seeing he previously faced him and barely escaped alive.

I never really understood as a child why Luke had to face Vader to become a Jedi. I knew that in the context of the Star Wars universe there had been other Jedi, and they hadn't needed to face Vader to earn that status. Thus, I was a little confused by this exchange between Luke and Yoda. It was later in life that I recognized the symbolism intended in the scene: Luke had to overcome his fear, for a Jedi is supposed to be without fear. Until he mastered his fear of Vader, Luke was not in fact a full Jedi. There is an interesting message in the idea that to overcome his fear, Luke had to face it. There are also interesting messages in the fact that to be a full-fledged Jedi (who were supposed to be the servants of the people) Luke had to overcome his fear, essentially choosing the light side and letting go of the dark side. Let's recall what we talked about above, that faith and fear cannot exist together. Fear goes hand-in-hand with doubt. I believe overcoming fear and overcoming doubt are also connected. There are some doubts that seem to tap into our deepest fears, which is why they can be the hardest to deal with and the hardest to overcome.

With this thought of facing up to our fears to overcome doubt, let's turn to Abraham's Trial of Faith as recorded in Genesis 22. Starting with verse 1, we read, "And it came to pass after these things, that God did tempt Abraham, and said unto him, Abraham: and he said, Behold, here I am." I'm going to pause here for clarity. It says that God "tempted" Abraham. My initial reaction to that expression is to wonder why God would encourage Abraham to do something wrong (because that's what I think of when I read the word "tempt"). However, it is interesting that the Hebrew word translated here as "tempt" can also mean "test or prove." Guess what? Here are those words again! We came across those words in the section the Definition of Faith. We've also dealt with them in this section, where we pointed out that the Trial of Faith *tries* our faith, meaning to test or prove it. We could reframe this by saying that God is giving Abraham an opportunity to prove that he would be as faithful with God as God was with him. God is not encouraging Abraham to do something wrong, but rather testing his resolve and commitment to being faithful to the commandments. Maybe we can look in general at the Trial of Faith as an opportunity to prove how faithful we can be: to choose the right and the light, and reject the darkness of fear and doubt.

OK, so let's read on to find out what test God will give Abraham as an opportunity to prove faithful: "And he said, Take now thy son, thine only son Isaac, whom thou lovest, and get thee into the land of Moriah; and offer him there for a burnt offering upon one of the mountains which I will tell thee of" (Genesis 22:2). That appears to be a direct command to offer his son as a human sacrifice. We just said above that God is not encouraging Abraham to do something wrong, but giving him an opportunity to prove faithful. And yet this command still has a feeling of being a requirement to do something wrong.

If we wanted to make a big deal of this, we would point to the aspect of sacrificing or killing a child. But remember that wasn't the point of the commandment given to Abraham. The commandment was more along the lines of Yoda's statement to Luke, that he had to face Vader to become a Jedi. The most important thing to me about this commandment is that it was *specifically for Abraham*. It was specific to him, and specific to a situation. We should not think it justifies any delusion to disobey God's general commandments because we think there's something contrary to the commandments that we want to excuse.

Our record in Genesis does not tell us how Abraham received the commandment from God. But we know that Abraham was very familiar with receiving communication from God, and *he* was certain it was a commandment from God. He had a track record of angelic visits, and other direct communication from God. We don't know the circumstances, and we don't have all the facts and details, so we need to accept that it was a commandment from God. As with everything we read in scripture, I can say whatever I want about it, but at the end of the day, it has to be between you and the Lord as to whether or not you accept and believe it. I know where I stand. I have studied, pondered, and prayed about this account. I do not understand all the circumstances regarding God's commandment to Abraham, but I am certain *Abraham* knew it was a commandment from God. Thus, *I* am certain it was a commandment from God, and we will look at the rest of the account with that in mind.

Back to our account, I brought up Star Wars at the beginning of this subsection because of the idea that Luke had to face up to and overcome his deepest, darkest fear. Sometimes the Trial of Faith causes us to face up to our fears; and when we do, we have to overcome the fear and the doubt to escape the Trial of Faith. The trials we experience in life can provide us exactly the circumstance we need to master our deepest, darkest doubts and cast them aside in favor of the light. Those who don't give up and give in will eventually win out against doubt (it will "come to pass"). Those who don't give up will fill their lives with light despite the concerns they experience and despite the Trial of Faith—and perhaps because of the Trial of Faith. Those that give up on the Trial of Faith will be left defeated by their doubts. There will be no peace in that. Abraham's account can teach us some of the things we'll need to know and do to keep on keeping on through the Trial of Faith.

To understand why this Trial of Faith is Abraham's "facing Vader" scenario for becoming free from doubt, we have to detour for a moment over to the Book of Abraham in the Pearl of Great Price. In Abraham 1:5–7, we learn that Abraham's people had "turned from their righteousness . . . unto the worshipping of the gods of the heathen. . . . For their hearts were set to do evil. . . . Therefore, they turned their hearts to the sacrifice of the heathen in offering up their children unto these dumb idols, and hearkened not unto my voice, but endeavored to take away my life by the hand of the priest of Elkenah." So we find out that when Abraham was a child, the people intended to slay him on an altar (see Abraham 1:12) to make a sacrifice of him to their gods.

We learn that Abraham's "father was led away by their idolatry" (Abraham 1:22), and determined to take away Abraham's life by idol sacrifice (see verse 30). Apparently, Abraham had been on the receiving end of a father trying to sacrifice a child to idol gods. I can only imagine what it must have been like to have a father who was going to sacrifice me to his god. That is sure to leave some emotional scars. I can imagine the experience left a deep, dark fear in Abraham. And now the God that Abraham had sought out and trusted to deliver him from his own father, who was about to sacrifice him (see Abraham 1:2–4, 15–17), that same God in whom Abraham trusted was requesting that Abraham offer up his son as a sacrifice on an altar. What's going on here? What must Abraham have felt? Just think about the feelings of betrayal (the betrayal of his own father in attempting to sacrifice him, and the betrayal of now doing the same, the betrayal of performing an offering that Abraham ascribed to the heathen). Think of the feelings of hypocrisy in now considering offering up his own son. There must certainly have been other emotions and doubts that would have flooded his soul as he considered obeying the Lord.

Returning to Genesis 22, remember that verse 2 indicated that the Lord would tell Abraham the mountain on which to offer the sacrifice, but maybe He didn't identify it at first. Then we read: "And Abraham rose up early in the morning, and saddled his ass, and took two of his young men with him, and Isaac his son, and clave the wood for the burnt offering, and rose up, and went unto the place of which God had told him. Then on the third day Abraham lifted up his eyes, and saw the place afar off" (Genesis 22:3). Three days is a long time to go looking for the mountain in these conditions. I imagine Abraham was hoping God would forget to specify which mountain so that Abraham could show up and say, "Well, I did what you asked, Lord. But I don't see the mountain, so I guess I'll take Isaac and go home now." Instead, for three days Abraham went to find that mountain, despite feelings of doubt and dread he must have been experiencing. For three days, he was probably wondering why he was obeying this request.

I start to think that three days is plenty of time to turn back. Three days is plenty of time for that small doubt to build into a large doubt. And this is one of the challenges with the Trial of Faith. It represents that time where we have to choose to not give up on the Trial of Faith. As we try to wait on the Lord, it becomes increasingly difficult to maintain the Focus of Faith and the Vision of Faith, and it becomes more difficult to cast aside our doubts. The longer we struggle with our challenges, the more our doubts can obstruct our view. Consider the doubt Abraham must have felt: on the one hand, we presume Abraham had learned to hear the Lord's voice, which was why he was on this journey to begin with; on the other hand, the Lord had promised to make Abraham a great nation through his son that finally came, and now the Lord was asking for his son back—so the rational mind asks how the Lord can possibly fulfill His promises.

There are doubts that deal with how much confidence we have in ourselves, or how we are confused over why it seems the Lord is not answering our prayers, or other such-things. And then there are doubts that cut to the core of our beliefs. Abraham surely felt strongly against the heathen sacrifices. Abraham surely was grateful and overjoyed at finally receiving the son through whom the Lord promised to raise up a nation. Now he was asked to sacrifice his only heir. I imagine this Trial of Faith cut to the core of Abraham's beliefs. Abraham had to face up to his deepest fears and doubts.

When our doubts are more than just trials, when they cut to the core of our beliefs and make it hard to even *want* to continue trusting, much less mustering the capability to keep trusting—isn't this when your nose hits the cold, hard wall? So how do we endure the Trial of Faith? How do we maintain our Vision of Faith when we are continually assaulted by doubt? How do we keep the Focus of Faith when our doubts cut to our very core? How do we maintain what we see with the Eye of Faith when everything tries to tell us it isn't true? How do we feel the Feeling of Faith and overcome every doubt, when our doubts cut deep into our primal emotions? The only answer I've been able to come up with is that we have to keep on keeping on. To keep on keeping on, we will have to draw on the assurances we've felt in the past that God has delivered us, to gain present assurance that He will deliver us again. We return to our anchor point of emotional assurance (our anchor of faith) to remind ourselves of what we've felt in the past. We return to the well of living water that springs from faith to drink again. We remember partaking of the fruit of the tree of testimony to bolster our motivation and desire to do so again.

We don't know what Isaac was thinking the whole time as they went out to where the Lord showed Abraham the mountain of sacrifice. But at last Isaac spoke up and asked the all-important question for the circumstance: "And Isaac spake unto Abraham his father, and said, My father: and he said, Here am I, my son. And he said, Behold the fire and the wood: but where is the lamb for a burnt offering?" (Genesis 22:7). Abraham's answer shows both his commitment to carry through with the will of the Lord, and his hope that the Lord would or did prepare a way for His word to be fulfilled. "And Abraham said, My son, God will provide himself a lamb for a burnt offering: so they went both of them together. And they came to the place which God had told him of; and Abraham built an altar there, and laid the wood in order, and bound Isaac his son, and laid him on the altar upon the wood. And Abraham stretched forth his hand, and took the knife to slay his son" (Genesis 22:8–10).

This record is a little scarce on the details, such as whether Isaac put up a fight, or how long Abraham took to prepare the altar, or how Abraham must have been pleading with the Lord to not make him carry through with the sacrifice. But here was Abraham's faith: he was sure of what the Lord had asked him to do, and he was committed to carrying through, no matter what would come of it—he would leave that to the Lord. That was Abraham's example. I think Abraham was able to fight off doubt by the assurance he had that the Lord had spoken to him. There are times in the Trial of Faith where the only thing that will keep us holding on is when we have felt deep in our soul with the Heart of Faith that the Lord has spoken to us. Only when we recall what we felt will we have the courage to carry through with our part, trusting that somehow the Lord will carry through with His.

And just at the moment that Abraham committed to obeying God, no matter what, the Lord stepped in. "And the angel of the Lord called unto him out of heaven, and said, Abraham, Abraham: and he said, Here am I. And he said, Lay not thine hand upon the lad, neither do thou any thing unto him: for now I know that thou fearest God, seeing thou hast not withheld thy son, thine only son from me. And Abraham lifted up his eyes, and looked, and behold behind him a ram caught in a thicket by his horns: and Abraham went and took the ram, and offered him up for a burnt offering in the stead of his son" (Genesis 22:11–13). Indeed, the Lord did provide the sacrifice. Incidentally, we remember that we worship a fourth-watch God. It was just at that moment when Abraham was fully committed to obeying, and not a moment sooner, when the Lord stepped in. It was just at that moment, and not a moment sooner, that Abraham showed the depth and quality of his faith. It was at the moment his nose hit the cold, hard wall that the purity of his faith-trust was evident.

Now think for a moment about the fact that God is omniscient. That means He knows *everything*. Since He knows everything, we must assume that He knew Abraham would obey. But significantly, *Abraham* did not know that Abraham would obey until that point in time when he committed to it. Abraham's Trial of Faith was not for God. It was for Abraham. It was for Abraham to "face Vader" and overcome his fear and doubt of committing to the Lord. Let's revisit something from earlier when we saw that faith is a two-way street and that the Trial of Faith can test both sides of that street. On the one hand, we must become committed to waiting on God's faithfulness. On the other hand, we prove to ourselves that we are as faithful with God as we have seen Him be with us. When we learn what the Lord wants us to understand, and as we become who the Lord wants us to become, the Lord ends the Trial of Faith. But we are left with a witness of God's power and faithfulness after the trial.

Referring again to what we learn from Abraham's example, I wonder how he found the capacity to continue on in the face of such a trial. What I feel deeply is what we looked at in the section the Feeling of Faith. Abraham trusted in the Comfort of the Lord's initial promises, Confident that the Lord has power to always fulfill His words, even when we can't see how He can. Abraham mustered up Courage by reflecting back on his initial Commitment to carry through with whatever the Lord asked him to do, and the experiences he had that generated that Commitment in the first place. We need to remember that commitment does not come in the hour of trial. Perhaps faith does not begin until our nose hits the cold, hard wall, but commitment can begin even before we take the first step toward it. Commitment is renewed as we focus on the Lord's promises, and the evidence we have seen of His power. Commitment leads to courage to continue when we think of giving up. Abraham was committed to doing the Lord's will. I think this allowed him to find faith and determination he probably didn't even know he had.

Abraham was rewarded for his faith: "And the angel of the Lord called unto Abraham out of heaven the second time, And said, By myself have I sworn, saith the Lord, for because thou hast done this thing, and hast not withheld thy son, thine only son: That in blessing I will bless thee, and in multiplying I will multiply thy seed as the stars of the heaven, and as the sand which is upon the sea shore; and thy seed shall possess the gate of his enemies; And in thy seed shall all the nations of the earth be blessed; because thou hast obeyed my voice" (Genesis 22:15–18). Abraham wasn't blessed for walking to the mountain. He wasn't blessed for hearing God's voice. He wasn't blessed for his words of hope and comfort to Isaac. He was blessed, the Lord said, "because thou hast obeyed my voice," and "not withheld thy son, thine only son." The trial will lead to blessings as we *obey*, willing to give everything up to the Lord, until the Lord says it is enough. Again, we wait to be "lifted up" as we talked about above.

In your Trial of Faith, expect the Lord to provide you with blessings. Some of those blessings will be the strength we gain and the things we learn about ourselves. Some will be the blessings we need to keep on trying in the Trial of Faith. The Lord knows everything and surely knows how we will act in our Trial of Faith. But we will learn a lot about ourselves. We can find faith and determination we did not know we had, which will help us keep our initial commitment to follow the Lord's voice in every circumstance. We have to put aside our fear of what might go wrong so that we can make way for courage to live in faithfulness for the blessings of faith to come into our lives. That is how we overcome every doubt. We at least momentarily put every doubt to the side to see instead what we can become by putting that doubt aside. As we replace doubt with faith, we actually become the person we need to be to fulfill the Lord's purposes and promises for us.

Through Trials We Reach Our Potential

There are many examples of the Trials of Faith recorded in scripture, so obviously we don't have the time to go through them all. We've covered a few that I find very interesting. But I think perhaps a discussion of the Trial of Faith would not be complete without talking about two other individuals whose trials seemed to go beyond anything else record in scripture: Job and Jesus Christ.

Whenever I hear about Job, I always hear about his faithfulness, but not the real feelings of challenge and difficulty that accompany the Trials of Faith he experienced. Job's experiences are interesting because I think we can set them out into different classifications of trial. I think most of life's trials can be categorized as one of the difficulties Job faced. There are challenges that cause us to lose our security and lose our temporal goods such as in Job 1:13–17, where violence and villainy by others caused Job to lose his wealth and earthly possessions. There are challenges based on harm or loss coming to our personal family like in Job 1:18–19, where a natural disaster caused Job to lose his children. At this point, Job expressed the understanding that possessions and relationships on earth are temporary, as he said: "Naked came I out of my mother's womb, and naked shall I return thither: the Lord gave, and the Lord hath taken away; blessed be the name of the Lord" (Job 1:21).

There are other challenges that we might experience in life, such as challenges suffered because of difficulty with our personal health as in Job 2:4–8, where Job was afflicted with painful sores all over his body. Still he retained his faith, and when his wife suggested that he "curse God, and die," Job instead "said unto her, Thou speakest as one of the foolish women speaketh. What? shall we receive good at the hand of God, and shall we not receive evil?" (Job 2:10). He testified that we are foolish to think that everything in life will go smoothly. But that statement by his wife introduces another challenge we may suffer: when those we love and trust do or say things that undermine our beliefs. Not only did Job receive such counsel from his wife, but his friends came to convince him that his suffering was punishment for his own wrongdoing. While they purported to come and offer him comfort, they became his accusers. Even through the midst of all the accusations and blaming by his friends, Job uttered a powerful testimony of what he believed in chapter 19: "For I know that my redeemer liveth, and that he shall stand at the latter day upon the earth: And though my skin worms destroy this body, yet in my flesh shall I see God: Whom I shall see for myself, and mine eyes shall behold, and not another; though my reins by consumed within me" (Job 19:25–27).

All of these types of challenges not only create stress and difficulty in life, they can actually cause us to challenge our own beliefs and struggle with our faith. But as Job illustrates, it is possible to maintain faith and integrity despite all of life's challenges. That does not mean that the challenges do not hurt us and test our trust in God. As we go carefully through the book of Job, we will find that he made several statements expressing his pain and confusion at the trials he was facing. I know I can relate to several of these statements; maybe you have also found yourself expressing similar feelings in your times of trial.

In Job 19:10, we read: "He hath destroyed me on every side, and I am gone: and mine hope hath he removed like a tree." I know I have expressed similar concerns, but it is important to keep in mind that deforestation in our field of trees of testimony will only happen if we give in to doubt. It is significant that this statement by Job comes just before his testimony about "in my flesh shall I see God," which we looked at above. Doubts come, and it is OK to acknowledge the hard time we're having, even if we are acknowledging how difficult it is to believe. But as long as we hold on to the things we know and keep on trying, we'll make it through our challenges.

In Job 23, we read: "Behold, I go forward, but he is not there; and backward, but I cannot perceive him: On the left hand, where he doth work, but I cannot behold him: he hideth himself on the right hand, that I cannot see him: But he knoweth the way that I take: when he hath tried me, I shall come forth as gold. . . . For he performeth the thing that is appointed for me: and many such things are with him" (Job 23:8–10, 14). There are times that it feels like we are doing everything we are supposed to do, and yet we still do not see the hand of God in our lives. But this statement by Job really moves me: after acknowledging that he cannot seem to find the Lord, he still testifies that God is taking care of him and leading him down the best path. Just because we cannot presently see God's hand, understand His doings, or feel His help, it doesn't mean that God is not aware of and guiding our circumstances.

It's great to have Job's example, but the fact is that it is extremely difficult to come to the point of expressing the faith and testimony he did when experiencing trial. As flawed beings, we tend to see through our own imperfect vision and we assume that God sees the same way we do. But Job's circumstance tells us more about the Vision of Faith. The fact is that we do not always know why we are suffering difficulty, and we do not know how long it will last. We continually look for reason or purpose for our trials, but sometimes we won't find an explanation for the sufferings we experience in life. In reading the book of Job, it does not appear that he was suffering in payment for sin, nor to learn something that the Lord was going to teach him (although he ended up learning from his experience). He was simply experiencing the negative side of life. There is not always an earthly explanation, but we tend to think there needs to be one.

Job and his friends exchanged a lot of back-and-forth exploring the "reasons" for Job's suffering. Job continued to claim his innocence to his friends, and his friends continued to accuse him of wrongdoing. But it was the "young man" of the group, if you will, that finally spoke, starting in Job 32. I believe that Elihu's overall message to Job is that Job lacks the proper perspective. In Job 33, Elihu teaches that we as men are not in a position to declare whether we "deserve" suffering or not, because we do not understand God's purposes in what happens in our lives: "Surely thou hast spoken in mine hearing, and I have heard the voice of thy words, saying, I am clean without transgression, I am innocent; neither is there iniquity in me. Behold, he [meaning God] findeth occasion against me, he counteth me for his enemy, He putteth my feet in the stocks, he marketh all my paths. Behold, in this thou art not just: I will answer thee, that God is greater than man. Why dost thou strive against him? for he giveth not account of any of his matters. For God speaketh once, yea twice, yet man perceiveth it not" (Job 33:8–14).

In Job 34, Elihu teaches that we should not look at life's sufferings as being unjust, even if they come from God. He also points out that God does not see a difference in a person based on material goods, which is significant at least because Job and his friends made arguments regarding Job's guilt or innocence based on his prosperity and fall from prosperity: "What man is like Job, who drinketh up scorning like water? Which goeth in company with the workers of iniquity, and walketh with wicked men. For he hath said, It profiteth a man nothing that he should delight himself with God. Therefore hearken unto me, ye men of understanding; far be it from God, that he should do wickedness: and from the Almighty, the he should commit iniquity. For the work of a man shall he render unto him, and cause every man to find according to his ways. Yea, surely God will not do wickedly, neither will the Almighty pervert judgment. . . . Is it fit to say to a king, Thou art wicked? and to princes, Ye are ungodly? How much less to him that accepteth not the persons of princes, nor regardeth the rich more than the poor? for they all are the work of his hands" (Job 34:8–12, 18–19).

Finally, in Job 35, Elihu teaches that God does not perceive as we do: "Thinkest thou this to be right, that thou saidst, My righteousness is more than God's? For thou saidst, What advantage will it be unto thee? and, What profit shall I have, if I be cleansed from my sin? I will answer thee, and thy companions with thee. Look unto the heavens, and see; and behold the clouds which are higher than thou. If thou sinnest, what doest thou against him? or if thy transgressions be multiplied, what doest thou unto him? If thou be righteous, what givest thou him? or what receiveth he of thine hand? Thy wickedness may hurt a man as thou art; and thy righteousness may profit the son of man" (Job 35:2–8).

In Job 37, we read: "Hearken unto this, O Job: stand still, and consider the wondrous works of God. Dost thou know when God disposed them, and caused the light of his cloud to shine? Dost thou know the balancings of the clouds, the wondrous works of him which is perfect in knowledge?" (Job 35:14–16).

The fact is that while God wants our righteousness, He is not troubled with, nor focused on material things. While He wants to bless us, maybe it is more important that He guide us. If we look only to success in material things and success in earth life as our measuring stick, we are not looking at life in the same way God looks at it. Job was humbled, and humbled himself before the Lord, recognizing that no amount of worldly success and wisdom can bring us to God's level or provide us with God's perspective. As hard as it may be, what we need most in the Trial of Faith is humility to endure the trial.

God sees this life very differently than we do, because it is all we really know while He knows there is so much more. He sees our potential. Our ultimate potential is perfection (see Matthew 5:48). Trial helps stretch us to our potential. But only One achieved the goal of perfection in this life—God's Only Begotten Son. While the New Testament records relatively little of Jesus's life and teachings, we can see that He experienced Trials of Faith. There is one sacred trial that I wish to refer to here, which is Jesus's time on the cross.

After spending hours on the cross, suffering pain, as well as the mocking from so many of the people, "Jesus cried with a loud voice, saying, Eli, Eli, lama sabachthani? that is to say, My God, my God, why hast thou forsaken me?" (Matthew 27:46). "Why hast thou forsaken me?" He asks, which suggests that Jesus felt alone or abandoned by His Father. Surely, living without sin, Jesus would have enjoyed the feeling of the presence of the Father throughout His entire life. He had never known such distance from the feeling of God's presence, for He knew no sin. And so it was not the trial in Gethsemane where "his sweat was as it were great drops of blood" (Luke 22:44); it was not with the lashings, the crown of thorns, or the humiliation at the hands of the soldiers; it was not when the people rejected Him in favor of a murderer; it was not as He carried His own cross, exhausted as He was; it was not when the soldiers drove nails through His hands; it was not in any of these things that He cried out that He had been forsaken. Rather, I believe Jesus's ultimate Trial of Faith was when the heavens withdrew themselves so that He might go through the valley of the shadow of death, alone. That is when He cried out (see D&C 122:8, 76:107). It was when Jesus's faith was tested by His Father withdrawing the Light that He had enjoyed His entire sinless life. And then He was required to be the Light. He was required to become what He was destined to become; to reach His potential. And in that moment of ultimate trial, He did what was required of Him. He succeeded.

There may be times we feel that we should receive more help from the heavens in some of our trials. Maybe it is at those times that the heavens train us to become what we are destined to become. While Jesus was required to pass that particular trial alone, He promised us, His disciples, in John 14:16–18, "And I will pray the Father, and he shall give you another Comforter, that he may abide with you for ever; Even the Spirit of truth; whom the world cannot receive, because it seeth him not, neither knoweth him: but ye know him; for he dwelleth with you, and shall be in you. I will not leave you comfortless: I will come unto you."

I truly believe that He gives that promise to all of us. And look at what it says: the world cannot receive the Spirit, "*because it seeth him not.*" But we know we will not dispute just because we do not see, or do not understand what the Lord has in store for us (see Ether 12:5–6). We will trust that the Lord will bless us with His presence through the Comforter. As we do that, while we still may not know why or how the Lord is directing us, we will trust that there is a purpose to our faith, even if there doesn't appear to be purpose to our suffering. We will trust, and even know, that all of life's experiences, especially the Trial of Faith, will guide us along the path of the Journey of Faith to the place of God's promises.

JOURNEY *of* FAITH

I'm amused that people, including myself, are so attracted to shiny and sparkly objects. In fact, the shinier, sparklier, and rarer an object is, the more we seem to like it. I assume that's why we have used "precious metals" as money and why jewels have long been symbols of status and wealth. One of the most popular gems is the diamond.

Diamonds are very interesting objects. Pure diamonds are made entirely of carbon atoms. That's it—pure carbon. Real diamonds tend to have impurities, but they are still almost completely carbon atoms with whatever impurities they contain. Interestingly, coal is basically also just carbon atoms. Diamonds are shiny, and coal is black. Why the difference between these two things when they are made of basically the same essential element? Well, we need to understand something about physics. Carbon atoms are able to form into different kinds of structures. The most common structure is a flat structure like a microscopic sheet of paper, which tends to form in layers. The sheets are relatively easily broken up into pieces. When found purely in layers, the carbon forms graphite (often used in pencils), which does have a sheen to it. Coal is very similar, with more randomness to its structure and hence a darker appearance. However, carbon atoms are also able to form a three-dimensional structure that has, interestingly enough, a "diamond" shape. The structure looks like two pyramids connected base-to-base. The three-dimensional structure is referred to in science as a crystal or lattice structure. This crystal structure results in an incredibly hard material that under normal conditions cannot be scratched or broken up by anything on earth except other diamonds.

Coal appears black because with the structure of the carbon atoms in coal, light enters easily and doesn't reflect back out. However, change that structure to a diamond structure, and something interesting happens. Light still enters very easily, because the diamond is clear. But because of the crystal or lattice structure of a diamond, the light bounces around inside of it, and gets trapped inside for a split second, bouncing around for a little bit before getting back out. As it bounces around, the colors of light get separated (think of a prism or a rainbow) and then join back together and repeat the process over and over before coming out. So light goes into a diamond like it would into glass, but with glass it just continues to go right through, and with a diamond it gets bounced around on its way back out. That splitting apart and bouncing around for a split second is the basic reason why diamonds are sparkly and glass is not.

Most elemental carbon ends up forming something like graphite or coal, and only forms into diamonds in just the right conditions. Those conditions occur deep inside the earth when just the right temperature and pressure exist and there is enough carbon available. Even when the right conditions exist, diamonds take a long, long time to form. Until then, we would think of the carbon as basically just coal. If the temperature and pressure are off, or if the temperature and pressure are right but there is no carbon, only rocks form. There would be no diamond.

Hold onto the diamond analogy for just a moment now while we remind ourselves what we've learned up to this point. We have talked about how to train ourselves to open our minds to see with faith. We have also seen what it means to have faith and how to live it, what we have to do to build our faith, and how that faith will be strengthened and proven. So up to this point we have focused on a lot of the details of faith. Now I want to take a look at the bigger picture of faith. I want to look at life as a Journey of Faith, with all these details helping us understand where we're headed, and why.

Coming back to diamonds, the journey of a diamond is to start as a lump of carbon (the right substance), be put through high pressure and temperature (the right conditions), and then to wait. The longer we wait, the bigger the diamond can become. But even then, a diamond must be refined to become the shining gem that provides brilliance to anyone who sees it. The Journey of Faith is meant to take us somewhere, just as faith is mean to make us something. We may feel that we start out as a "lump." But you and I and every other person on this planet are the children of God (see Romans 8:16), so we are the right substance. Based on what Jesus said to His disciples, we can understand that our divine potential is to become perfect as our Father in Heaven is perfect (see Matthew 5:48). Our potential is to receive all that is light and good, let it bounce around inside and illuminate us, and then return it to the world, having enlivened us with brilliance like a diamond. The process may require high pressure, waiting, and eventually a refining, such as that encountered by the Trials of Faith.

If we apply our faith in God through the process, the pressures we face in life will form just the right conditions to allow God to turn us into a diamond. Without that application of faith, we risk becoming nothing more than a lump of coal or a rock, hardened and common, lacking in brilliance to share with the world.

I think I have always had a vague notion that having faith is a good thing, and very important. But despite the fact that it is the first principle of the Gospel of Jesus Christ, I think I mostly just had a vague understanding that it would bring me "blessings," whatever that was supposed to mean. As we have been learning, faith is something far more understandable, and far more powerful than a vague "I believe" feeling that takes me I-don't-know-where. The question I now want to explore is this: What good is faith? What happens to us when we gain real faith, the kind of real faith we've been talking about?

When I had two small children, someone I knew told me his view on parenting, which still influences my approach to parenting years later. He said that parenting is the process of turning responsibility for a child over to the child. I find that to be extremely profound. We are not strictly caretakers, although that is something necessary. We are not strictly rule-makers or disciplinarians, although those are also important roles of a parent. We are not simply teachers, or even examples, because there is something more profound and personal we need to accomplish with parenting. To me the best kind of parent is one who will take their children and try to help them turn into the best version of themselves that they can be.

I believe God is our Heavenly Father. I believe He acts as a Father, and my experience has been that He is the best kind of parent. I believe that our divine destiny is to acquire celestial attributes as God has. I believe our faith relationship with God is the process by which God helps us turn into the best version of ourselves. Our Journey of Faith is to take on a mortal life and learn to rise above our mortal experience as we acquire celestial character. Faith, if you will, is a path from where we currently are to eventually a better version of ourselves and ultimately to the perfect version of ourselves.

Reflect on the previous section, the Trial of Faith. In many cases the Trial of Faith helps move us along the path in the Journey of Faith. Now let's talk about how to keep making progress on the Journey of Faith, even in the face of distraction. I think the following story can teach us something about evaluating where we are in the Journey of Faith and how misunderstanding and taking things for granted can distract us from our journey. Let's revisit one of the stories we've already seen—the story of the brother of Jared and the people of Jared leaving their home to get to the promised land. However, we're going to look at a different part of that story here.

I remember being intrigued, even when I was young, by hearing people tell of how the brother of Jared "forgot to pray for four years." While the story appears to suggest that, I wonder if there is a more complete description of what took place. In Ether 2, we first read of the people starting the journey to the land of promise that the Lord had promised them. Then we read: "And the Lord would not suffer that they should stop beyond the sea in the wilderness, but he would that they should come forth even unto the land of promise, which was choice above all other lands, which the Lord God had preserved for a righteous people" (Ether 2:7). The first important thing to recognize is that the Lord wanted them in the promised land, and He didn't want them stopping until they got there.

The people clearly knew that the Lord had promised to take them somewhere. In verses 8–12, we read about what the

Lord had promised regarding the land He was taking them to. Then we come to this: "It came to pass that the Lord did bring Jared and his brethren forth even to that great sea which divideth the lands. And as they came to the sea they pitched their tents; and they called the name of the place Moriancumer; and they dwelt in tents, and dwelt in tents upon the seashore for the space of four years" (Ether 2:13). Remember how we talked about repetition earier? See how the phrase, "they dwelt in tents" is repeated here? Why is that repetition significant? It tells me that the people knew they hadn't arrived at the promised land, because they dwelt in tents there for four years. If they had thought they had arrived at the promised land, surely they would have started to construct real houses and buildings, right? And if they knew that they hadn't arrived at the promised land, they should have followed the Lord's direction and kept moving until they got there. The fact that they didn't tells me they were stalled on the path to the promised land.

Taking their story as my story, I know I personally can get distracted when trying to get to where the Lord wants me to go. I wonder if that's what happened to them here. They knew they were supposed to be getting somewhere, but stalled out on some nice beachfront property. I see in my mind that they were having the weekly bonfire down on the beach, collecting shells to make jewelry and maybe setting up sandcastle building contests. They had experienced some trials and difficulties getting to this point, and now they had the good life and weren't in any hurry to get on to where they were supposed to go. This visual depicts all the reasons I can imagine having stalled out on the beach if it had been my journey.

In that context, we read the following: "And it came to pass at the end of four years that the Lord came again unto the brother of Jared, and stood in a cloud and talked with him. And for the space of three hours did the Lord talk with the brother of Jared, and chastened him because he remembered not to call upon the name of the Lord" (Ether 2:14). I don't really know whether the brother of Jared didn't pray at all. The way I see it, he was the prophet, and had been close to the Spirit, and even here in chastening him, the Lord was talking to him. I suspect that maybe he offered some prayers that sounded something like: "please bless that we'll have a good day," or "please bless this food," and maybe even other more meaningful prayers. But there was obviously something missing in his prayers for the Lord to come down and chasten him for forgetting to pray. Maybe he didn't pray with real intent.

I think the next verse might offer some insight into what his forgetting-to-pray sin was in this situation: "And the brother of Jared repented of the evil which he had done, and did call upon the name of the Lord for his brethren who were with him. And the Lord said unto him: I will forgive thee and thy brethren of their sins; but thou shalt not sin any more, for ye shall remember that my Spirit will not always strive with man; wherefore, if ye will sin until ye are fully ripe ye shall be cut off from the presence of the Lord. And these are my thoughts upon the land which I shall give you for your inheritance; for it shall be a land choice above all other lands" (Ether 2:15).

Did you see it? It says that when he repented, he "called upon the name of the Lord *for his brethren*," which suggests that maybe he hadn't been doing that sufficiently before. Perhaps that is what he had forgotten all that time. He was not praying as a leader should pray, for the care and guidance and well-being of those he had been called to lead. Perhaps he hadn't been praying for specific guidance on how to achieve the will of the Lord that he knew about, which specifically was how to get to the land of promise. And the Lord says two things to him: the Spirit will not always strive with man, and these are my thoughts about the land of promise.

Whether the brother of Jared prayed for some things, or for himself only, or not at all, I think his sin of not remembering "to call upon the name of the Lord" was that he and his people were supposed to be getting somewhere, and he wasn't doing what was needed to lead them there. "And the Lord said: Go to work and build, after the manner of barges which ye have hitherto built. And it came to pass that the brother of Jared did go to work, and also his brethren" (Ether 2:16). Now that he was reminded what he needed to do, the Lord wanted him to get on task. I don't know if they started right away, because it says "and it came to pass that" they got to work.

Returning to my imagined visual, maybe the brother of Jared protested something along these lines: "I understand we're supposed to get to the promised land, but we've been traveling for so long—can we not just rest for a bit? This is a good land, and we want to stay and enjoy it! Maybe we can just let everyone think we have arrived at the promised land for a while so they can feel the stability of belonging somewhere." Sometimes we get caught up in living. Sometimes we're so busy with prosperity that we don't find time to get to work on getting to the promised land. Maybe even after we are reminded to get to work, it comes to pass that we get around to it. We can enjoy prosperity so much we forget that the Lord has bigger plans for us.

Or maybe the issue was the opposite of prosperity. Maybe instead of getting caught up in how well things were going, they were simply bogged down in how hard it was to live there. Maybe the brother of Jared protested something along these lines: "You say we need to go to the promised land, but we've got people who are sick, and we have women who are pregnant. Are we really expected to get pregnant ladies onto boats? To get in the boats we'll need provisions, and we can hardly find enough food and water as it is. And all these storms and insects—as soon as we get started we get stalled again by the weather or the bugs." Sometimes we're so busy with the trials and difficulties of life that we're working so much to battle the trials that we forget to put effort into putting ourselves in a circumstance where the Lord can take us to the promised land.

In either case, this people had stalled out, whether from prosperity or trial, and had stopped making the Lord's journey. I know I've stalled out for both reasons at different times in my life. Just like the Jaredite people, I had to get up and get back to work to resume following the Lord's appointed path. The Journey of Faith takes us from testimony to testimony, from trial to trial, from blessing to blessing, and from strength to strength. However, I think we sometimes "remember not to call upon the name of the Lord" to know where all of this is supposed to be leading us. I would guess that you believe your faith will take you to the presence of God. But are you getting there, and how would you know if you were? Are you integrating your faith into every aspect of your life as you, in all things, move closer to the land of promise, or are you distracted making sandcastles and collecting shells, or distracted keeping out of the wind and rain so that you stop moving forward? The sandcastles do not last forever, the shells do not have the value of the things that await you in the promised land, and the winds and rains can actually drive you to the promised land.

So where does the Journey of Faith lead? The simplest answer is that it leads to where the Lord wants to take us, which may not be where we had in mind. It might be that we come across some beachfront property, set up our tents, and hope the Lord forgets to tell us that it's time to move on. As we travel on the Journey of Faith, we should remember that we are bound for the promised land and that it is infinitely preferable to any mansion that we could dream up for ourselves. It can be hard to remember that especially since we aren't quite sure where it is. But the Lord knows the way, and He asks that we follow Him.

A Journey of Action

We discussed in the section the Definition of Faith that action on our part is one of the distinguishing factors between true faith and a mere profession of belief. *Lectures on Faith* states: "Faith [is] the first principle in revealed religion, and the foundation of all righteousness" and "the principle of action in all intelligent beings." Also, "faith is not only the principle of action, but of power also, in all intelligent beings, whether in heaven or on earth."[1] Faith is a principle of action. I think that is the primary message James provided in James 2: "Even so faith, if it hath not works, is dead, being alone. Yea, a man may say, Thou hast faith, and I have works: shew me thy faith without thy works, and I will shew thee my faith by my works" (James 2:17–18). As we start looking at this, let's be clear that the subject of works and its relationship with faith could probably fill its own book, especially because that would really require us to also study grace since our works always come short of the glory of God. A study of grace would naturally lead to a study of Christ's Atonement, and so forth. Our purpose here is not to address the subject of works generally, but is more of a specific discussion of how the idea of works helps us understand how to take the Journey of Faith. In short, we are talking about "action," which is the expression Joseph Smith used. I think James's "works" refers to the same thing Joseph Smith was talking about when he said faith is the principle of action. Let's look at more of James 2 to provide some context to this discussion.

"What doth it profit, my brethren, though a man say he hath faith, and have not works? can faith save him?" (James 2:14). Here is another series of questions like we discussed earlier in the account of the father who lacked faith. What are we invited to evaluate here? James asks if faith can save a man. More specifically, he ponders the circumstance where we say we have faith but do not back that up by how we act. I think James is asking: "Does it benefit a person to profess faith but not act in accordance with that profession? If there's no action behind the words, does the person professing faith become anything?" In short, I think James is asking us to consider what kind of faith saves a man, and how such faith is manifest.

Once again, recall that *faith* is derived from words implying trust and trustworthiness or faithfulness. The first question sets up a paradox: If someone says they trust, but then their actions or works are not consistent with that profession, is that actually trust? Is that actually faith? Instead, I think such a profession could be thought of as more of an intention to trust, or an intention to be faithful. I think James illustrates this intent to have faith with his example: "If a brother or sister be naked, and destitute of daily food, And one of you say unto them, Depart in peace, be ye warmed and filled; notwithstanding ye give them not those things which are needful to the body; what doth it profit? Even so faith, if it hath not works, is dead, being alone" (James 2:15–17). The person saying "depart in peace" *intends* good things upon the one suffering. But good intentions do not address the needs of the individual, and so do not help the one suffering. Similarly, James tells us, intention alone is not faith that will save us. Intention alone is not action, but merely a false start on the Journey of Faith—maybe like getting on our bicycles and not pedaling when we intend to go up a hill. As we discussed earlier, faith is about commitment and courage, which are both defined by how we act when our faith is put to the test. Action frames the commitment and courage that intention alone lacks.

James makes this point with his conclusion: "Yea, a man may say, Thou hast faith, and I have works: shew me thy faith without thy works, and I will shew thee my faith by my works" (James 2:18). The phrase "thou hast faith" refers to the person discussed above who professes faith but does not act in a way consistent with the profession. Such a person can never prove faithful. Such a person can rightly be challenged to prove their faith. James explains that how we act (our works) is the proof of our faith.

James then explains that works give life to our faith. "Was not Abraham our father justified by works, when he had offered Isaac his son upon the altar? Seest thou how faith wrought with his works, and by works was faith made perfect? And the scripture was fulfilled which saith, Abraham believed God, and it was imputed unto him for righteousness: and he was called the Friend of God. Ye see then how that by works a man is justified, and not by faith only. . . . For as the body without the spirit is dead, so faith without works is dead also" (James 2:21–26). You can reread this entire discussion of James's teachings, replacing the word *works* with the word *action*.

I think we can understand that Abraham's faith caused him to act the way he did ("faith wrought with his works"), and by acting the way he did, his faith was perfected ("by works was faith made perfect") as he saw the hand of the Lord work in his life. This example is a very good summary of the Journey of Faith—we believe in God's word, and so we act in a way that shows we believe it to be true. God delivers on His word, strengthening our trust that He will be faithful in the future.

There is no Journey of Faith without the right works. Said another way, there is no progress in the Journey of Faith without action. We act and work and believe, which takes us down the path of the Journey of Faith. Without the kind of faith manifested by action, we are simply chasing a dead-end, seeking for strength from something that has no power to take us where the Lord wants us to get. We will make no progress on the Journey of Faith, but instead will eventually find ourselves stalled out in a familiar, comfortable place, like the Jaredites on the beach, making sandcastles that will eventually be washed away by the tide.

So faith is the principle of action. Joseph Smith also said that faith is a principle of power. I think that faith is a principle of power at least because faith empowers the one who has faith. Faith is a source of strength. As we saw in the Trial of Faith, there are times when our trials will exhaust our own strength, and we will be left to draw strength from our faith. That faith can let you know that God is there, mindful of your journey. The Journey of Faith will invariably lead through stormy seas, or over mountain heights, or across the valley of sorrow, or out in the barren wilderness. However, we can be empowered to take our journey, knowing that God will be with us wherever He wants us to go. Ultimately, it is by trusting that we will be empowered, which can help overcome fear and doubt to begin to act in the way we will feel in our hearts that we should.

Hope Drives the Journey

To this point we've gone through a lot of discussion about the subject of faith, but there is something that we have glossed over until now. The concept of hope is used in all the scriptural "definitions" of faith that we've looked at (Hebrews 11:1, "faith is the substance of things *hoped for*, the evidence of things not seen"; Alma 32:21, "faith is not to have a perfect knowledge of things; therefore if ye have faith, ye *hope for* things which are not seen, which are true"; Ether 12:6 "faith is things which are *hoped for* and not seen" [emphasis added]). So our understanding of those definitions probably isn't complete until we look at hope. I don't think we can have a complete picture of faith without understanding why faith appears to be defined in terms of hope.

The funny thing is that when I look for a definition of hope in scripture, I find it only in combination with reference to faith! Moroni 7 includes the following: "And again, my beloved brethren, I would speak unto you concerning hope. How is it that ye can attain unto faith, save ye shall have hope? And what is it that ye shall hope for? Behold I say unto you that ye shall have hope through the atonement of Christ and the power of the resurrection, to be raised unto life eternal, and this because of your faith in him according to the promise. Wherefore, if a man have faith he must needs have hope; for without faith there cannot be any hope" (Moroni 7:40–42). After reading this, it seems to me that faith is defined in terms of hope, and hope is defined in terms of faith. It appears we must have faith to have hope, but we have to have hope to have faith. How do we unravel the circle?

I got the feeling that the expression *hope* has a somewhat different meaning in scripture than it does as commonly used in modern language. As we did above with the word faith, I decided to look at the origin of the word hope to see if that could help my understanding. Interestingly, the origin of the word hope appears to be unknown. I guess we'll just have to fall back to the dictionary definitions of the word to see what they can tell us. Different definitions of *hope* that I have seen include the following uses: to wish, to wait for, to expect, or to anticipate.

Let's just think through what each of these expressions means and see if we can tease out a common thread. The following are my takes on the definitions above. When we "wish" for something, we engage in some sort of dreaming, wanting something to happen, but we may or may not have a basis for thinking it will happen. A wish is ephemeral.

When we "wait for" something, we know it will take time, but we are willing to hold on until it happens because we think it will happen. We wait passively by just going about our lives content to see whether or not it comes to us. We wait actively by preparing for it, and counting down the days or hours until it actually comes to pass. We may do something to prepare for it.

When we "expect" something, we feel that something is deserved or due. When we expect something, it seems illogical to think that it won't happen. When I expect something, I tend to think that I am done "waiting for" it, and that the thing is going to happen soon, or at least within some measurable time. When we expect something, we are more clearly prepared to do something to get ready for it.

Similar to expecting something, when we "anticipate" something, we have great confidence that it is going to happen. We look forward to when it will finally happen. We may be on edge because we have yet to experience the thing we are waiting for, but have committed ourselves to it so fully that in our minds it might as well have already taken place. I cannot imagine anticipating something without having done something to prepare for it. In my mind, anticipation means I expect something to happen, and the question is just how soon it will happen.

When we look at what all of these uses have in common, we see that with hope we look forward to something that hasn't happened yet. The different uses of hope might separate based on how much confidence we have in the thing that hasn't happened yet, or how much basis there is (how reasonable it is) to think it will occur. Even though wishing is only one definition of the word *hope*, my sense is that hope as used in modern English frequently means wishing. But in scripture, I think the expression *hope* refers to something about which we can have confidence—there is a basis for thinking or believing something will happen. Thus, I like the concepts of "expect" and "anticipate" when looking at hope in scripture. We have reason to expect something, and it is just a matter of when and how the thing will come to pass. We will do something to prepare for it. I also want to add the concept of "longing" to our waiting. To me, just as scriptural faith carries feelings with our trust and understanding (the feeling are the "four C's" as we talked about above), I think scriptural hope carries the feeling of longing with the anticipation.

With this in mind, let's look back at Moroni 7:40–42. Verse 40 asks, "[How can we] attain unto faith, save [we] shall have hope?" There are a number of ways we can understand this verse in light of what we've already discussed. One simple way to understand is to ask: "How can we trust God, unless we can look forward to His promises?" The answer, of course, is that we can never learn to trust until we learn to let go and wait upon the Lord, and look forward to things that have not yet happened. There is no trust where the thing has already happened.

Verse 41 inspired the title of this subsection: "And what is it that ye shall hope for? Behold I say unto you that ye shall have hope through the atonement of Christ and the power of the resurrection, to be raised unto life eternal, and this because of your faith in him according to the promise." Again, let's look at this verse in light of what we've learned. What do we anticipate or hope for? Verse 41 gives the answer, which we can reorder like this: We hope to be raised unto life eternal—this is what we look forward to, even though we know we cannot achieve it alone; the basis we have to expect to be raised to life eternal is that God made a promise; we expect to activate that promise of eternal life through faith/trust in Christ; and, we feel assurance that we can activate such a promise because of Christ's Atonement and power of the Resurrection.

We could say that hope provides a destination. It provides us a goal to look forward to, if you will. It gives a direction for our acts of faith. It illuminates the Vision of Faith and the Eye of Faith. For this reason, hope drives the Journey of Faith, because what we hope *for* shows us where we're headed, and what we hope *in* shows us how our faith is going to get us there.

After that discussion, verse 42 sounds a little clearer to me. It says that if we come across a person that has faith as described in scripture, that person necessarily has hope, because that person had to obtain a vision of the destination, and had to accept the basis of a promise to get there as well as the assurance that the destination is reachable. The person had to be able to gain the trust that identifies scriptural faith to expect to reach the promised destination. So we can understand that we have to have hope and use it to "attain unto" faith.

And what does the last part of the verse mean? I think it tells us an important truth about the relationship of hope and faith: faith can only be born through hope, but hope cannot be sustained without maturing into faith. Let's repeat that, because it could be a little hard to follow the first time: faith can only be born through hope ("if a man have faith he must needs have hope"), which means that faith doesn't start without generating hope in something. However, hope alone isn't enough, because hope cannot be sustained without maturing into faith ("for without faith there cannot be any hope"), meaning to keep the expectation of the thing we hope for, we will need to create and act on faith. Faith cannot exist without hope, but hope cannot survive without faith. Why? Let me illustrate with the following story.

I went on a camping trip with my family when my four girls were ages twelve, ten, six, and four. I had the idea to do a little hiking, which turned out to be more difficult for my kids than I expected at the outset. Still, we found our way to the top of Saddle Mountain in northwestern Oregon. We took it easy at our campsite the next day, but were interested in doing another little hike—we had a pamphlet that told us the hike was only a mile on a trail that wasn't very difficult, and this one went to a lake, so we thought it would be fun to do. It turns out we somehow had misinformation about that "little" hike, which turned out to be about 2.5 miles one direction and rated as "difficult."

We started off excited to get to the lake. We brought very little in the way of snacks or water, because we expected to get there in about thirty minutes or so. After hiking for about forty minutes on much tougher terrain than we anticipated (the kind where we had to carry the four-year-old almost the whole way), we expected the lake would be right around the next bend or up the next little climb. After another ten minutes, everyone's tension was increasing, and the hike stopped being fun. If only we could make it to the lake so that our effort would not be lost! But after over an hour of hiking, we turned around, defeated.

We came across something interesting on the way back. My oldest daughter found a piece of paper on the trail, which she opened to reveal a map of the trail we were on. It clearly indicated 2.4 miles and a rating of "difficult" to get to the lake.

When we started on the hike, we had an incorrect understanding of what lay ahead of us. We did not pass anyone else on the trail who could have provided the correct information to us. Our expectation to make it to the lake in thirty or forty minutes was impossible under the true circumstances. It turns out our hope was really just a wish, because the basis for our expectation was faulty. We had no real basis to expect it. Our determination to make it to the lake disappeared as we went further and further past what we thought we had to do to get to the destination. When we finally turned around, we had no hope and no determination to find the lake.

Our hope at the beginning of the hike was to reach the lake. Our faith was represented by our willingness to hike the trail. Our hope, our interest in the "Lost Lake" destination, was what initially inspired us to go on the hike. We can see that our faith was generated from our hope. However, faith based on misinformation cannot produce power. When it became clear to us that somehow we were deceived in trusting that we could reach the lake in a reasonable amount of time with a reasonable amount of effort, we lost our faith. (Incidentally, I find it ironic that this happened on the way to Lost Lake!) We really stopped trying. As our faith waivered, our hope to reach the lake turned into apathy—our lack of faith destroyed our hope. So, without hope there cannot be any faith, and without faith hope cannot survive. We do not act without an expectation of a benefit or without moving forward from our action, and we cannot expect to reach our expectation without focused action.

In light of understanding this relationship between faith and hope, let's revisit Hebrews 11:1 ("Now, faith is the substance of things hoped for, the evidence of things not seen") as: Now faith is the foundation of things you long for and anticipate happening, the evidence of things you expect to happen, which have not happened yet. Let's also revisit Alma 32:21 ("And now as I said concerning faith—faith is not to have a perfect knowledge of things; therefore if ye have faith, ye hope for things which are not seen, which are true") as: And now as I said concerning faith—faith is not to have a perfect knowledge of something; therefore, if you trust in God (and His words/promises), you long for something that hasn't happened yet, but which you have basis to know will happen, and which you expect to come to pass.

We should always be careful about taking creative license with the language of scriptures, so as not to substitute our language for the Lord's language. However, sometimes as a little exercise it is helpful to try to look at the same thing we've seen over and over in a different way to help us consider deeper understanding. For me, this exercise shows that using "anticipate" and "longing" as an understanding for hope is consistent with the use of "trust" and "evidence" as an understanding of faith.

Now let's go back to Moroni 7:41: "And what is it that ye shall hope for? Behold I say unto you that ye shall have hope through the atonement of Christ and the power of the resurrection, to be raised unto life eternal, and this because of your faith in him according to the promise." We hope through the Atonement of Christ to be raised up to eternal life. That is ultimately the Journey of Faith: to become perfect through God. We will find that we will not go through life and suddenly get put into a happy place (like some imagine our reward of heaven to be), and there we are, happy forever. I believe heaven is about achieving our potential, which is to become perfect and therefore become like God. We will continue on that journey until it is achieved. Faith will take us along the path to what we hope for, what we long for with great anticipation and expectation.

Recall the scriptures we discussed earlier when discussing faith in terms of hope, Hebrews 11:1, "Faith is the substance of things hoped for, the evidence of things *not seen*"; Alma 32:21, "Faith is not to have a perfect knowledge of things; therefore if ye have faith, ye hope for things which are *not seen*, which are true"; Ether 12:6, "Faith is things which are hoped for and *not seen*" (emphasis added). As indicated this time, each verse refers to faith being in things "not seen." We have learned previously that faith requires us to learn to wait patiently on the Lord. But why is faith not faith if it is seen? As we talked about above, faith can mature into testimony, or surety. But when faith starts, it is based on not having a perfect knowledge. Remember that as soon as something is seen, there is no longer faith because there is knowledge of the thing. We experience and see through faith until we have testimony and knowledge, just as the brother of Jared had so much faith that he saw God and knew Him. I would submit that a testimony or a sure knowledge in one area is strongest when it is obtained through the process of trust and growth required by faith. Then sure knowledge in one thing can inspire further faith in other areas.

Interestingly, Paul discussed hope in a similar way in Romans 8:24–25 with the following: "For we are saved by hope: but hope that is seen is not hope: for what a man seeth, why doth he yet hope for? But if we hope for that we see not, then do we with patience wait for it." Notice how he said we do not see it, and so we wait for it with patience. But why is hope not hope if we see it? If hope is about anticipation, but we have seen the thing we anticipate, there really isn't anything to look forward to, is there? Maybe you've also had the experience of receiving a gift, which was supposed to be a surprise, which you somehow found out about prior to the presentation of the gift. No matter how good you are at pretending to be surprised, the fact is that the *actual feeling* of anticipation, and therefore the actual feeling of surprise, has already passed. Even if you can act it, you won't feel it. Similarly, with scriptural hope, when the thing we might anticipate is already here or when the thing we would anticipate is assured to us no matter what, we cannot feel the anticipation and longing for it. We cannot rejoice in the destination and we cannot rejoice in taking the journey if we are already there or assured to be there with no effort on our part. That produces no motivation and no drive to take the Journey of Faith. In fact, there is no Journey of Faith, because we do not have to go anywhere or become anything to get there.

Before seeing more of Paul's words, let's go back to Boyd K. Packer's description of the Leap of Faith: "Somewhere in your quest for spiritual knowledge, there is that 'leap of faith', as the philosophers call it. It is the moment when you have gone to the edge of the light and step into the darkness to discover that the way is lighted ahead for just a footstep or two."[2] If hope is the destination, and faith takes us on the path to that destination, let me suggest the following: hope tells us there is something out in the dark that is worth obtaining; and faith is the trust that if we step out into the dark we will be led to it. So, which one, hope or faith, stirs us to action? Can we really separate them?

It is true that we could charge out into the dark not sure we will find anything, simply because we have the spirit of adventure (a fool's hope). Our faith in that case is only that we will have an adventure—it is really blind faith. We could also charge out into the dark *hoping* to find something without *trusting* that we ever will. In that case, our faith will waver quickly, and our hope will be exposed as mere wishful thinking. But when we have basis through the word of scripture or the inspiration of the Holy Spirit to believe something is out past the darkness, as we finally trust enough to step out into the darkness, the path is lit by obedience, and hope and faith work together to keep us moving along. As we have faith to take further steps, the light will appear those precious few steps in front of us.

Now let's go back to Paul's words in Romans 8: "Likewise the Spirit also helpeth our infirmities: for we know not what we should pray for as we ought: but the Spirit itself maketh intercession for us with groanings which cannot be uttered. . . . And we know that all things work together for good to them that love God, to them who are called according to his purpose" (Romans 8:26, 28). The Spirit calls us out into the unfamiliar and lights our path as we obey His promptings. Even when we "know not what we should pray for as we ought," the Spirit can guide us. We just need the hope that there is something there, and a few steps prompted by the Spirit of the Lord can be enough to keep us on the journey. The reason we step out into the dark to begin with is that we believe Paul's affirmation that "all things work together for good to them that love God." I think scriptural hope is born from a love of God. That love gives us the reason to hope, or to anticipate that which we do not yet see. I believe that if we want greater hope, we will find it by getting to know God better, because that is how we will learn to love Him more. Try putting more effort into scripture study and prayer, and ask God to help you know Him better. Your love will grow, and you will be filled with hope to take the Journey of Faith.

God Is the Rewarder of Them That Seek Him

If you lived in my Oregon neighborhood, you might have seen me in my shorts and running shoes out for a jog. I would typically run a couple of times a week, which could have you believing that I like running. And it is true—I do like running, but perhaps not in the way you might expect. I would set goals for my running (e.g., a certain pace or a certain distance), and push myself to reach those goals. I honestly enjoyed the challenge of mastering myself and pushing my personal capacities, so I enjoyed running partly for those reasons. But really I went running because I have a passion for soccer. I played indoor soccer for years. We didn't have "practices," but would show up and play a game each week. I found that by keeping a regular routine of running and other exercise, I performed better at soccer. When I fell out of my routine for even just a couple weeks, I developed sluggishness in my legs and had a greater chance of getting injured. I occasionally even felt bad enough that I didn't feel like going to play soccer, which I am normally very enthusiastic to do. I am sure I could get into running as an activity in itself, but its primary purpose in my life was to serve to prepare me for what I really wanted to do—play soccer.

Maybe you also have goals that really serve as steps to get to something else you are really interested in. One interesting thing about this is regardless of why we have the goals, if we work toward them, we tend to receive the benefit of them. For example, if I run so I can play soccer better, or if I run because I want to run, I enjoy both the physical and psychological advantages of regular exercise. I am healthier for my efforts and able to play soccer better, even if I do not ultimately reach my running goals. It is the effort that I put into reaching those goals that fulfills the true purpose I had for running.

We've discussed above how hope can identify an object of our faith or a goal of our faith. We also discussed how faith is built on an expectation that a promise will come to pass. We might naturally want to start thinking of all the things we want to have happen, to make "faith goals" out of all those things. But maybe the goals of faith are more like my running goals—maybe they are not the things in and of themselves that are the ultimate purpose behind those goals. As we take a larger perspective view at the Journey of Faith, we may find that sometimes we did not understand the Lord's timetable for a particular promise, or we find that our perspective on how things will work out is not always the same as the Lord's perspective.

Recall that Paul the Apostle taught about faith in his Epistle to the Hebrews. His audience was believers in Jesus Christ that came from a Jewish background—a people to whom the Lord had sent prophets and had made many, many promises. Some of those promises had been fulfilled, and some had not yet come to pass. Some that had been fulfilled had taken a long time (generations in many cases) in being fulfilled. These Christian converts Paul was addressing were making a transition from the old law (law of Moses) to the new law (Jesus's law of the gospel), from strict performance to the path of faith. Naturally, the longer we travel on the path of the Journey of Faith, the more we want the fulfillment of that which we hope for. But just as the history of this people shows, fulfillment of the Lord's promises frequently doesn't come when we would like. I think Paul addresses this concern in Hebrews 11. But he also affirms that the process of Living Faith, of seeking after the Lord, provides rewards in itself.

We've talked about the first couple of verses multiple times already, but we need to start with them again to understand what Paul is teaching here: "Now faith is the substance of things hoped for, the evidence of things not seen. For by it the elders obtained a good report" (Hebrews 11:1–2). Remember that hope is something we anticipate and long for, and faith is related to trust and faithfulness. Recall also that substance here refers to assurance or foundation, and evidence is proof, as in proof we obtain by putting something to the test. With all of this in mind, we get the following. Our trust and faithfulness is the assurance that the thing we anticipate and long for will actually happen or be achieved. Our trust and faithfulness is proof of where we are trying to get or what we anticipate. By our trust and faithfulness, we obtain a testimony.

Now I want to continue to the next verse: "Through faith we understand that the worlds were framed by the word of God, so that things which are seen were not made of things which do appear" (Hebrews 11:3). So, verse 1 tells us faith gives us assurance and proof of things not seen, and verse 2 tells us a testimony comes through faith. Verse 3 then tells us that we understand something by faith. We understand that the "worlds were framed by the word of God," which I believe refers to the Creation. Through faith, we understand the Creation or the setting up of the universe and that it came by the word of God. Then Paul says this fundamental understanding leads to understanding that "things which are seen were not made of things which do appear."

Notice that the language he uses in verse 3 ("things which are seen") is a parallel to the language of verse 1 ("evidence of things not seen"). And remember from above that the "evidence of things not seen" refers to the "things hoped for." Paul is tying the "things hoped for" to the Creation. We talked before how Paul wanted the Romans to understand that there is great power in the word of God (recall our discussion of the subsection Faith Comes by the Word of God). Consider that through the word of God, the worlds were framed together. That is the power of the word of God. We did not see that happen in our lifetime, but we can see right now that the worlds are framed together.

Now consider that the "things hoped for" have not yet happened in our lifetime ("for what a man seeth, why doth he yet hope for?" [Romans 8:24]). But if we hope for something because of the word of God (for example, we believe a promise received through the word of God), we can trust in the same power that framed the worlds together to carry out the Lord's promises that we hope for, which have not yet been fulfilled. The same God that has the power to create the universe has power to fulfill all His promises. The evidence of things we can see right now can provide assurance of the things that have not yet come to pass. That is what we're invited to trust in. We can have a testimony that God will carry through on what He has said. We have an even stronger testimony that He will bless us as we seek after Him in the way He has said.

There is more to discuss in verse 3. First, let's take a look at the word "appear." An appearance is always from a perspective or a point of view. Even if we refer to angelic visits in scripture and say an angel "appeared," we understand that the angel did not materialize out of nothing. Rather, the angel existed, but was not visible to the individual because of the state of mortal existence of the individual seeing the angel. When God framed the worlds for mortal life, He placed things in a physical, mortal state. How things appear to us right now is not how they appear to God, for He has a perfect understanding of all things, and we are limited to how we experience things in this mortal state.

When Paul says that "things which are seen were not made of things which do appear," I believe he's asserting that the things that come to pass by the word of God do not necessarily come to pass in ways that we will comprehend. We cannot find an explanation for everything by what we see in front of us or what we observe in our mortal state. We cannot limit our hope to mortality. Through faith, we can reach beyond what appears possible to us now. Even as we see the earth, man's study through science continues to present as many questions as it appears to answer. Given that our perception is limited to the mortal state in which we are placed, if we limit ourselves to physical observation, we will always be limited to understanding how things appear from the perspective of our mortal realm. This is also true of our understanding of God fulfilling His promises—we are limited in our understanding to how things appear from our perspective.

If we cannot understand all of how God fulfills His promises, what are we supposed to understand? When Paul says "so that," I think it means he invites us to take what we know (by the word of God the worlds were framed) and extend it to the fulfillment of the word of God in other areas. Let's say that the things which are seen are the fulfillment of the word of God. Through faith (by living in faith and seeking after the promise), we understand that the fulfillment of our faith is not made of things as they appear to us. Through Living Faith, we see the fulfillment of promises in ways that seem incomprehensible to our imperfect perception. And yet when we pay attention, we see that the Lord does lead us to the fulfillment of His promises as we seek after them in faith.

Now we come back to the trust aspect of faith. Man's observations will always leave us missing some of what is really there. Since we do not see the complete picture, we must trust that God's purpose and plan will be fulfilled, despite how things might appear to us. Even though we saw that hope can identify the destination of our faith, and faith is what takes us on the path to reach the destination, in the Journey of Faith, we typically have several expectations that we think "should" happen along the way to the ultimate promised outcome. However, God sees a more complete picture, and what may appear to us as "the path" to the thing we hope for is not always the path God has in mind.

I have found that the path as it appears to me is rarely the path God has in mind for me. Perhaps this is a little like my running goals—the goals are great in and of themselves, but ultimately, even if I do not meet them exactly as I planned, I can still become a better soccer player. Notice also that my running goals can be very identifiable, but "playing soccer better" is more of a pursuit, or something to seek after, or a process of becoming something. We need not get hung up on *our expectations* of what we think should happen on the Journey of Faith, trusting that God's ultimate purpose is to take us where He wants us to go, to become what He wants us to be.

So how do we trust in God's ultimate purpose when we may not understand what that is, or how He wants to take us there? Through the Eye of Faith, we open our minds and hearts to see the promises that come through the word of God. Then we act, which opens and creates the path of the Journey of Faith to the object of our hope, which is the thing we see with the Eye of Faith. And we will find that as we diligently seek the object of our hope in God's way, we will actually be seeking God's will. Then we will find that God is the rewarder of them that diligently seek Him.

Let's say it this way: the Journey of Faith is a journey of trust or faithfulness, which is a path from where we are now to when God will fulfill His promises, and to what we will be when He does. Faith creates in us the conditions for reaching our goal and transforms us as we take the path towards our goal. Our actions (our faith-acts) assure us that our goal is reachable, and prove that we will reach it, as long as we continue down the path. As we have already talked about with respect to patiently waiting on the Lord, we do not control *when* we will reach the promised destination or when or how God will fulfill His promises. But what we can do is continue to move along the path and by our faith-acts become who we should be to arrive at that destination. We cannot take the Journey of Faith without changing ourselves. The change itself provides the rewards of diligently seeking the Lord, even before reaching the destination; and even if we don't see the fulfillment of the promise in this mortal life.

Recall that faith is a principle of power in all intelligent beings.[3] I suggested above that faith is a principle of power at least in part because faith empowers the one exercising it. Now also let me suggest that faith has power to create a path from where we are to the thing we hope for. We hope for something because we accept the word of the Lord, whether by a promise from scripture, or by living prophets, or by the word of the Spirit to our hearts. When we pay attention, we see that all the Lord's promises carry an invitation for us to *become* something and adopt more godly behavior. Every promise to receive a gift or blessing from the Lord is also an invitation to prepare ourselves so that we can accomplish greater things and serve better when the gift or blessing is received. We begin faith by accepting the word of the Lord, including the invitation to become something more, not casting it away through skepticism. We act on the word of the Lord, which begins the Journey of Faith. Our actions both show our trust and faithfulness and increase them, and the path opens before us. This is like what we talked about above where we take the Leap of Faith and the way is illuminated for just a couple of steps in front of us.

Now recall that in verse 2, we saw that "obtained a good report" can mean to obtain a witness or testimony. In light of the Journey of Faith, God gives us testimony that we are on the path to the destination of the thing hoped for. When we know we are on the path, with God as our ally, His testimony that we are achieving our goal can be as powerful as any other form of knowledge. Even though we have not yet seen the fulfillment of the thing we hope for, that testimony can be almost as strong as seeing that fulfillment. There are other blessings we receive besides testimony, which enrich and improve our lives. We, like those before us who have put faith to the test, can obtain witnesses of God, His faithfulness, and His power. Such testimony fuels our flame of assurance that God will deliver on the promised goal or destination as we progress towards it with faith.

One more reflection before we move on with the rest of Hebrews 11. We've just talked again about the fact that faith requires action on our part. Again, I want to stress something important about faith and action. Faith is defined in terms of faithfulness, which is a measure of how well we do at behaving the way we have committed to act. And yet, faith is not *about* our actions, in and of themselves. If we fail to understand this, we'll wind up chasing after blessings and we'll be disappointed when they don't show up every time we do something right. With faith, our actions show our faithfulness and also our trust. We perform whatever actions we perform because we trust that once we get on the Lord's path, He will guide and bless us with His wisdom. With faith, we seek the Lord's wisdom, not our own desires. God, in His infinite wisdom and mercy, blesses us along the way in ways that we expect, as well as in ways we do not. So, true faith requires our actions, but it is not strictly about them.

In verses 4 and 5, Paul tells us of two individuals that received blessings for their faith: Abel and Enoch. "By faith Abel offered unto God a more excellent sacrifice than Cain, by which he obtained witness that he was righteous, God testifying of his gifts: and by it he being dead yet speaketh. By faith Enoch was translated that he should not see death; and was not found, because God had translated him: for before his translation he had this testimony, that he pleased God."

While we are not told specifically here what promises the Lord had made to Abel and Enoch, we learn that, among other things, they received a witness that they pleased God by seeking after Him through their faith.

Paul affirms that seeking God through our faith is the way to please God and receive His blessings: "But without faith it is impossible to please him: for he that cometh to God must believe that he is, and that he is a rewarder of them that diligently seek him" (Hebrews 11:6). The New Testament has many passages, most of them from Paul, that teach us that salvation comes through faith and grace, not by works (meaning merit on our part). And here he explains that we use faith to diligently seek after God. In return, God, through His grace, rewards us for seeking. Notice that we don't have to "find" Him to receive rewards, just seek diligently. I can witness that the more we seek God, the closer we come to finding Him, and the greater the blessings we receive. Similarly on the Journey of Faith, we apply our faith to seek after the things hoped for and not seen. As we do, we receive the rewards of our mature tree of testimony.

After the story of Abel and Enoch, Paul gives several examples of people who sought after God and His promises. "By faith Noah, being warned of God of things not seen as yet, moved with fear, prepared an ark to the saving of his house; by the which he condemned the world, and became heir of the righteousness which is by faith" (Hebrews 11:7). I think "moved with fear" refers to Noah's acceptance of the Lord's promise that destruction would come. Noah anticipated the Lord's word would come to pass, and anticipated with apprehension (hence, "fear"). Whether we expect blessing or destruction based on the Lord's promises, the important part is to act with faith.

"By faith Abraham, when he was called to go out into a place which he should after receive for an inheritance, obeyed; and he went out, not knowing whither he went" (Hebrews 11:8). Notice that he wasn't even sure where the Lord was leading, and still he was willing to follow. "By faith he sojourned in the land of promise, as in a strange country, dwelling in tabernacles with Isaac and Jacob, the heirs with him of the same promise: For he looked for a city which hath foundations, whose builder and maker is God" (Hebrews 11:9–10). Here we see that Abraham sought the promised land, just as the Jaredites did. We see that Abraham had a vision of a "city which hath foundations, whose builder and maker is God." I think it is very significant that Abraham envisioned a promised land that God would build, and which God would guide him to. Thus, Abraham didn't need to know where the promised land was to seek after it. I think there are times the Lord will allow us to try to find a way towards His promised blessings before allowing us to see them, and there are countless blessings for us in learning to seek.

There is also a great lesson in the next thing Paul points out. Recall that Abraham was promised that his descendants would be innumerable, but then he and Sara lived out their childbearing years with Sara being barren. Surely the Lord's promise could not have made sense. How can your descendants be countless in number, when you have no children through whom to have countless offspring? And yet God showed that He can do His own work. Sara and Abraham apparently never lost faith that God could carry through on His promises. "Through faith also Sara herself received strength to conceive seed, and was delivered of a child when she was past age, because she judged him faithful who had promised. Therefore sprang there even of one, and him as good as dead, so many as the stars of the sky in multitude, and as the sand which is by the sea shore innumerable" (Hebrews 11:11–12). Despite the fact that from every mortal perspective Sara was past the point of being able to have a child, somehow, they kept their faith, and by keeping the faith they were blessed with a child. One child is hardly a countless number of descendants, but they did not doubt. They stayed focused on faith.

Paul doesn't go into detail on the subject, but I have pondered how it is that we can keep our faith even when it appears that there is no way for the promise to be kept. I used the word *appears* on purpose in that sentence, to point back to Paul's teaching that God does not necessarily fulfill His promises, or create the things we see, from how things *appear* to us. To me, the question of how we can keep our faith when it seems impossible is answered by understanding that God works from a different perspective than what our mortal minds comprehend. Namely, if we want to keep our faith that God will carry through on His promises, even when it seems all possibility is past, we have to try to see the situation how the Lord sees it. Seeing how the Lord sees is essentially always hard. Sometimes we won't be able to see it at all. But if we hold onto the promise, recognizing that the Lord does His work, we will be like those Paul identifies in the next verse: "These all died in faith, not having received the promises, but having seen them afar off, and were persuaded of them, and embraced them, and confessed that they were strangers and pilgrims on the earth" (Hebrews 11:13).

To me, this is one of the points Paul is trying to make in this chapter. Again, the Hebrews are the people to whom the Lord had made numerous promises, not all of which had been fulfilled. Some were fulfilled (like the coming of the Messiah) and the people in general didn't recognize it, because they did not understand God's work. But there were faithful ones that saw the promises of God afar off, even when the promises were not fulfilled in the desired time frame or in the expected way. Some even died before the Lord came through on His promises, and yet they "were persuaded of them." They died in the faith that God would carry out His work. I think we confess that we are "strangers and pilgrims on the earth" when we recognize that there is more to life than what is observable from a mortal perspective. We embrace the promises not just by dedicating ourselves to doing what is necessary to prepare ourselves to see them fulfilled, but by dedicating ourselves to allowing the Lord to do His work according to His wisdom.

The fact that God fulfills His promises, even when the fulfillment comes later, is something the Hebrews could understand based on their history. Paul recounts their history in the next few verses to guide their understanding: "For they that say such things declare plainly that they seek a country. And truly, if they had been mindful of that country from whence they came out, they might have had opportunity to have returned. But now they desire a better country, that is, an heavenly: wherefore God is not ashamed to be called their God: for he hath prepared for them a city" (Hebrews 11:14–16). The Jewish people understood the significance of a promised land, seeing that they had gone in and out of captivity and been led back into the land of their forefathers on occasion after captivity that resulted from disobedience and forgetting God. These people to whom Paul refers, who in faith would declare that they seek a spiritual country, a promised land, echo the declarations of the Jewish people throughout history. They sought the land or the country promised by God. But "if they had been mindful" and put their trust in God from the start, "they might have had an opportunity" to return to their land. As it was, the promise of inheriting the land was only fulfilled to later generations. Thus, the promises were fulfilled, but on the Lord's time and in accordance with His will and wisdom. Now Paul makes his point: The people with faith that he refers to also seek a country, or the promised land as the Jewish people sought. But these promises they seek are spiritual promises for a heavenly city prepared for them by God.

As Paul just explained, not everyone saw in life the city they sought after. But everyone who seeks is blessed and rewarded. In the next few examples, we can identify the hand of God in the lives of the people who sought a blessing, even when it did not come as they might personally desire it. Going back to Abraham, Sara conceived when she was past the age, and so it seemed that God's promises were being fulfilled. But then came Abraham's Trial of Faith, which we already discussed above. Paul said: "By faith Abraham, when he was tried, offered up Isaac: and he that had received the promises offered up his only begotten son, Of whom it was said, That in Isaac shall thy seed be called: Accounting that God was able to raise him up, even from the dead; from whence also he received him in a figure" (Hebrews 11:17–19). Paul points out that Abraham willingly offered up Isaac, his only begotten son, even though he had received promises from God that his offspring would be countless in number.

Here is a depth of faith we should all strive for: to see the *apparent* fulfillment of a promise the Lord has made, and then to receive a command or a prompting that *appears* to take away from that promise, and then to obey anyway. What did Paul say was Abraham's faith? That perhaps God would raise up Isaac from the dead so the Lord's promises could be fulfilled. Maybe a miracle is needed. Maybe something will have to happen that I do not understand. Regardless of what needs to happen, my faith needs to be as Abraham's, which is to trust the Lord's promises even when it means obeying His voice in a way that *appears* to me to be contrary to the promise. Such faith is to obey every word of God, trusting in His wisdom over ours. And developing such faith is part of the Journey of Faith.

We know that Abraham was blessed by the hand of God with divine intervention. Isaac was spared, and went on to bless his sons, Jacob and Esau, "concerning things to come" (verse 20), which Isaac did not see fulfilled in his mortal life. Jacob blessed the sons of Joseph (verses 21 and 22) with blessings he did not live to see fulfilled. Then Paul recounts some of the story of Moses (verses 23–29) who was blessed as he sought to lead the children of Israel at the Lord's command. Incidentally, some of the Lord's earlier promises to Moses were fulfilled as a numerous people went forth to inherit the land promised to the forefathers. However, recall that Moses himself wandered with the children of Israel for forty years, and eventually saw the promised land from afar, but did not get to go into it (see Deuteronomy 34:1–4).

Back to Hebrews 11, Paul then recounts other known heroes (verses 30–32) of Israel's past who lived under a law of performance and ordinances (the law of Moses), and yet fulfilled the Law of Faith. These individuals all acted in faith, trusting God to fulfill His promises. They acted in faith, and were blessed, even though the blessings came in unexpected ways (for example, when the walls of Jericho fell in verse 30). And what did all these heroes have faith in? Remember that Paul says they understood they were strangers on earth, preparing for the higher promises of the Lord. When we seek after and prepare for the higher promises of the Lord, we accept that our role may not involve seeing the fulfillment of the Lord's promises in the flesh in our lifetime. Even so, we need to be ready to seek, receive, and trust the Lord to bless in His time.

Paul recalls the heroes of the past: "Who through faith subdued kingdoms, wrought righteousness, obtained promises, stopped the mouths of lions, Quenched the violence of fire, escaped the edge of the sword, out of weakness were made strong, waxed valiant in fight, turned to flight the armies of the aliens. Women received their dead raised to life again: and others were tortured, not accepting deliverance; that they might obtain a better resurrection: And others had trial of cruel mockings and scourgings, yea, moreover of bonds and imprisonment: They were stoned, they were sawn asunder, were tempted, were slain with the sword: they wandered about in sheepskins and goatskins; being destitute, afflicted, tormented; (Of whom the world was not worthy:) they wandered in deserts, and in mountains, and in dens and caves of the earth" (Hebrews 11:33–38).

Notice that many received blessings in this life, while others acted in faith despite experiencing trials instead.

Significant to Paul's message, they all lived and died under the law of performances, and yet lived through faith. Maybe even more significant was that through their faith they lived the words of promise they had received, not relying on what *appeared*, but putting their trust in Him who had made the promises. Many died without the appearing of the thing they hoped for, but were still blessed by their faith and faithfulness to the Lord's promises. Their testimony of God's faithfulness and power did not come through the ordinances, but through their faith: "And these all, having obtained a good report through faith, received not the promise: God having provided some better thing for us, that they without us should not be made perfect" (Hebrews 11:39–40).

I think verse 40 can mean several different things, and I think one of them is that the Saints to whom Paul was writing were finally seeing the fulfillment of some of the promises to their forefathers ("God having provided some better thing for us"). Their forefathers worked in faith for something that was only fulfilled much later. The completion of the promises, and the perfection of the faith of those individuals, came when the promises were fulfilled to a later generation through Jehovah, the author and finisher of their faith. But note that they "obtained a good report through faith," which is the same language as verse 2 above, which refers to receiving a testimony of the work through faith, or maybe we can also say receiving a testimony of the work *of* faith.

Paul brings his writing full circle. In verse 1, he introduces the concept of faith as the substance of things hoped for. In verse 2, he says it is through faith that testimony is received. In verse 3, he explains that the promises we rely on in faith can be fulfilled in ways outside of our mortal perspective. In verse 6, he says that God rewards those that seek Him through faith. He gives numerous examples of people who acted in faith and received testimony and blessing. Then in verse 39, he explains that all who acted in faith received a testimony through faith, even though some did not see the fulfillment of the promises they hoped for in this life. But verse 40 assures us that the better thing the ancients sought for was fulfilled to later generations. It is beautiful language, and it offers an even more beautiful message. Surely this can buoy up our faith to seek after the Lord on the Journey of Faith. We will receive testimony that we please God, even if we do not see certain promises fulfilled. We are blessed in numerous ways as we find the path and change our nature to seek after the Lord and His promises. The blessings we do receive give testimony that God is faithful, and that we are on the right path in the

Journey of Faith. God is indeed the rewarder of them that seek Him. We diligently seek Him through our faith-acts.

We Obtain Witnesses along the Way

Once when my wife and I were on vacation, we had an opportunity to participate in a treasure hunt. We met at a starting point with other groups and received a map of the city and the first clue. The treasure hunt was supposed to run us around to various locations in the city looking for clues to eventually make our way to a restaurant for lunch. Each time we found a clue, we had to decode it to figure out where to go to find the next clue. As you can imagine, it was a lot of fun, but there were plenty of opportunities to get lost. We made a couple of wrong turns that had us wandering far off the correct course. Our primary reason for straying was that at one point near the beginning of the treasure hunt, we passed over one of the locations we were supposed to visit, and so missed one of the clues. However, the treasure hunt itself had a flaw in it, and we stumbled onto the next clue location and received a clue we were not supposed to obtain yet. The lack of the missing clue prevented us from being able to finish the treasure hunt, and the organizers had to find us and guide us to our lunch destination.

The Journey of Faith can be a little like that treasure hunt. Our treasure hunt promised to take us to a destination that was unfamiliar to us; we didn't know how long it would take to get there, and we didn't know ahead of time what path we should take. Our Journey of Faith is based on a promised destination that frequently we won't know how long it will take us to get there. We can often envision the destination of our

Journey of Faith, even though we aren't actually familiar with the destination or the path. As with the treasure hunt, there are plenty of chances to take a wrong turn on the Journey of Faith, and sometimes we may stray far enough that we won't be able to find the path again without some intervention. On the Journey of Faith, each part of the journey will teach us and challenge us and cause growth that we will need if we expect to reach our goal. Just as my wife and I missed a clue that prevented us from completing the treasure hunt, if we miss the growth and challenge on the Journey of Faith, we risk not arriving at the destination, because we will not become what we need to be to arrive there.

My wife and I began our treasure hunt on an assurance that something we hoped for was out there for us to arrive at (lunch), and each clue gave us further proof or evidence that the destination could be reached. With the Journey of Faith, we start with an assurance of what we hope for (the promise through the word of the Lord), and each act of faith on our part provides further evidence (or testimony) that we can achieve the goal. In fact, like the treasure hunt's clues at various locations, the Lord gives us testimony at various points along the Journey of Faith to assure us that we are on the right path. Each of these little testimonies adds to our field of testimony trees.

The clues received at each stage of the treasure hunt sustained the treasure hunt. The assurances and witnesses represented by the clues provided the path in our treasure hunt journey. Similarly, each witness we receive that God has sustained or rewarded our faith becomes an assurance that provides the path of the Journey of Faith. The witnesses received along the way sustain the Journey of Faith. We initially trust in something, and as our basis for trust is proven, our faith is strengthened and our hope deepened. I believe that Ether 12 can teach us about the witnesses received as we seek diligently after the Lord and His promises.

Ether was commanded of God to preach to a society that had lost its way. In Ether 12:3, the prophet taught "that by faith all things are fulfilled." We then read: "Wherefore, whoso believeth in God might with surety hope for a better world, yea, even a place at the right hand of God, which hope cometh of faith, maketh an anchor to the souls of men, which would make them sure and steadfast, always abounding in good works, being led to glorify God" (Ether 12:4). In verse 5, we read that Ether preached many things, "which they did not believe, because they saw them not." And then we read: "And now, I, Moroni, would speak somewhat concerning these things; I would show unto the world that faith is things which are hoped for and not seen; wherefore, dispute not because ye see not, for ye receive no witness until after the trial of your faith" (Ether 12:6).

We talked about all these verses above in the section the Definition of Faith. Let's just briefly recap some of the things they teach. Verse 3 affirms that every promise God ever makes will be fulfilled. Verse 4 teaches that when we put our trust in God, we have assurance of a better world. Verses 5 and 6 teach us that we obtain a witness through faith, and we must act before the witness will be given. In the previous subsection, God Is the Rewarder of Them That Seek Him, we saw that we must become something through faith before the thing we hope for can be fulfilled. Thus, we often cannot receive a witness until after the Trial of Faith. Hence, we commented above on Moroni's counsel: we don't have to see an immediate end result to make our conviction to live right—in fact, we *cannot* wait for an end result. Don't discount God's promises because you haven't seen them fulfilled, because the fulfillment comes after faith is exercised.

After verse 6, we see that Moroni goes on to identify a lot of instances of people exercising faith. I have heard since the time I was young that Ether 12 is "about faith." Of course, I had also heard that Hebrews 11 was generally "about faith," and we just saw that we can understand some specific messages from that chapter. Similarly, I believe there is at least one specific message for us in Ether 12. Paul points out that God rewards those who diligently seek Him. For me, Moroni wants us to understand about obtaining witnesses, which will fill in our picture of faith in a way that we will understand the path of faith—from the seed of faith to the tree of testimony.

In a curious parallel, the key to understanding Paul's point was to read verse 6 in light of the last couple of verses of Hebrews 11, and the key to understanding Moroni's message is also to read verse 6 in light of the last couple of verses of Ether 12. In Ether 12:6, Moroni introduces the idea that we must expect the Trial of Faith prior to receiving a witness. In verse 39, Moroni testifies that he spoke face to face with Jesus, and in verse 41, he admonishes us to "seek this Jesus of whom the prophets and apostles have written." I believe Moroni's point is that we can have a witness of Jesus Himself and His work, and he encourages us to seek that witness.

In light of this understanding, the examples Moroni provides take on a different light for me. Right away we can see that perhaps the examples of faith provided are meant to show how we can receive that specific witness of the Savior. We read: "For it was by faith that Christ showed himself unto our fathers, after he had risen from the dead; and he showed not himself unto them until after they had faith in him; wherefore, it must needs be that some had faith in him, for he showed himself not unto the world" (Ether 12:7). What is the point and the ultimate purpose of our faith? I submit that it is to bring us to Christ. We need to pass through many experiences, reach many things we hope for, and obtain many witnesses prior to coming fully to Christ, but that is the ultimate goal. My wife and I would not have gotten lunch on our treasure hunt by figuring out the location of the first clue or the second clue and then staying where we had arrived. The path unfolded with each clue, and we were meant to take that path. Similarly the path of the Journey of Faith unfolds with each experience, each witness obtained, and each tree of testimony planted. We are meant to continue moving on the path.

To really open our understanding to Moroni's message in Ether 12, I want to jump for a minute to Moroni 7, which recounts a letter from Mormon, Moroni's father. If Moroni wrote the Book of Ether while he was alone, I believe he must have already had his father's letter prior to writing Ether 12. I believe the content of Moroni 7 influenced Moroni's own teachings in Ether 12. In Moroni 7, Mormon started by talking about how to recognize good from evil, and how "every thing which inviteth to do good, and to persuade to believe in Christ, is sent forth by the power and gift of Christ" (verse 16). Then Mormon asks, "And now, my brethren, how is it possible that ye can lay hold upon every good thing?" (verse 20).

I think this question is the pivotal point of the chapter. It explains why Mormon spends the entire first part of the chapter talking about discerning between good and evil. He had told the people that he would speak on faith and "the way whereby ye may lay hold on ever good thing." And "the way" that Mormon refers to is faith and the exercising of it. Specifically, Mormon teaches that we gain the presence and influence of the Holy Ghost according to the power of our faith in Christ, by which God's promises are fulfilled (verse 32). He also teaches that "[if] ye will have faith in [Christ] ye shall have power to do whatsoever thing is expedient in [him]" (Moroni 7:33).

But Mormon doesn't stop his explanation there. Rather, he explains that faith is tied to hope, which we have discussed before. And finally, Mormon explains that faith and hope are "vain" unless we have charity. So, to recap, Mormon says that by discerning good and evil, we can tell what is good and in discerning what is good we will want to have all good things come to us, which will bring us to Christ. By faith in Christ, we can obtain all good things. We hope through faith, and we exercise faith based on our hope. But there is no point of hope or faith, or no point to obtaining any good thing, unless we embrace charity and meekness. To me, that sounds a lot like what we discussed in the Journey of Faith section—that the Journey of Faith takes us to something we hope for, but that we must *change* to be able to make the journey. So, all good things will come through Christ, with faith, hope, and charity. Let's take that understanding back to Ether 12. As we'll see below, Moroni doesn't just address some generic "faith" in Ether 12; he actually talks about faith, hope, and charity, and receiving witnesses.

"But because of the faith of men he has shown himself unto the world, and glorified the name of the Father, and prepared a way that thereby others might be partakers of the heavenly gift, that they might hope for those things which they have not seen. Wherefore, ye may also have hope, and be partakers of the gift, if ye will but have faith" (Moroni 7:8–9). On a first pass through these verses, I can understand that Christ prepared a way for us to have hope through faith. He also prepared a way for us to "be partakers of the heavenly gift," but it is not stated in the scripture what that means. There is somewhere else in scripture where the expression "the heavenly gift" appears—Hebrews 6:4–6 reads: "For it is impossible for those who were once enlightened, and have tasted of the heavenly gift, and were made partakers of the Holy Ghost,

And have tasted the good word of God, and the powers of the world to come, If they shall fall away, to renew them again unto repentance; seeing they crucify to themselves the Son of God afresh, and put him to an open shame." Here Paul talks specifically about those who apparently cannot be renewed or redeemed. So what is "the heavenly gift," which once received makes it so we cannot be redeemed afterward if we fall away? That starts to sound like "the heavenly gift" is a sure witness of Christ (see Alma 39:6, where we see that the crime of denying the Holy Ghost "is a sin which is unpardonable"). This means Moroni is telling us that Christ has prepared a way for all with faith to receive a sure witness of Him. I wonder how often we consider that to be the point of our faith, or the end goal of our exercises of faith? How would it make a difference in your life if you considered that more often?

In keeping with the ideas Moroni presents about being partakers of the heavenly gift, we see in Ether 12:10–11 that he talks about ministers of the Priesthood and the law of Moses: "Behold it was by faith that they of old were called after the holy order of God. Wherefore, by faith was the law of Moses given. But in the gift of his Son hath God prepared a more excellent way; and it is by faith that it hath been fulfilled." Let's think about this for a moment; the law of Moses was given by faith, and therefore provided a way to prepare men to receive "the heavenly gift." And that gift is the Son of God: "But in the gift of his Son. . . ." Those exercises of faith through keeping commandments and ordinances prepare us for receiving our sure witness of the Savior.

But without that exercise of faith, we cannot reach the gift, as we next read verse 12: "For if there be no faith among the children of men God can do no miracle among them; wherefore, he showed not himself until after their faith." Again, we see that Moroni talks about Christ showing Himself *after* the faith of the children of men. God prepares the law and calls those that can guide us to the goal or fulfillment of the law. I believe the ultimate fulfillment of all of the laws God has revealed through His prophets is that sure witness of Christ and the power that comes to our lives when we can fully commit ourselves to that witness.

However, there are some things that need to happen to receive that witness, and I think Moroni's examples identify those as well. "Behold, it was the faith of Alma and Amulek that caused the prison to tumble to the earth" (Ether 12:13). We frequently hear of sin being compared to bondage, and there is the parallel throughout the Old Testament where the children of Israel first fell into the bondage of sin, and they were then taken into physical bondage by their enemies. So, the story of Alma and Amulek can serve as a symbol or metaphor for the breaking down of the bondage of sin by faith. When we seek freedom from the bondage of sin, we are ready for the next step: "Behold, it was the faith of Nephi and Lehi that wrought the change upon the Lamanites, that they were baptized with fire and with the Holy Ghost" (Ether 12:14). Once we have repented, we can feel the cleansing and purifying fire of the Holy Ghost to make us truly free.

As if to reiterate the examples above, Moroni identifies that "it was the faith of Ammon and his brethren which wrought so great a miracle among the Lamanites" (Ether 12:15). What was that great miracle? Taking a people who did not know God and bringing upon them with the power of conversion through the Spirit such that they laid down the weapons of their rebellion and would no longer fight against God or men. These people developed such a faith and witness in God that they would do anything to avoid sin. Isn't that ultimately the purpose of all miracles—to bring souls unto Christ, and for them to gain a conviction to seek God and avoid sin? And so,

Moroni helps us understand that "yea, and even all they who wrought miracles wrought them by faith, even those who were before Christ and also those who were after" (Ether 12:16). All miracles are performed through faith. Faith is the power behind the miracles, and it takes us on a journey from sin and disbelief to a witness of Christ. That is the ultimate Journey of Faith—to secure a sure witness of Christ.

In my treasure hunt, my wife and I went from clue to clue to ultimately arrive at lunch. The Journey of Faith takes us from witness of one good deed or of one truth, to another and another, and ultimately to arrive at Christ. Moroni provides us with examples of the type of witnesses the faithful can receive. He first presents the account of the three Nephite disciples: "And it was by faith that the three disciples obtained a promise that they should not taste of death; and they obtained not the promise until after their faith. And neither at any time hath any wrought miracles until after their faith; wherefore they first believed in the Son of God" (Ether 12:17–18). The promise they received was that they should not taste of death. The witness we receive through faith is that we will be raised to eternal life and avoid spiritual death. A sure witness of Christ gives us a firm assurance that we will be raised to eternal life and exalted. Once again, Moroni repeats that no miracle is wrought until after faith. This is a repeated concept and as such it is imperative for us to understand. We don't get anywhere on our spiritual journey without faith.

We already talked about verse 19 when we discussed the Eye of Faith, which allows us to envision the object of our faith: "And there were many whose faith was so exceedingly strong, even before Christ came, who could not be kept from within the veil, but truly saw with their eyes the things which they had beheld with an eye of faith, and they were glad." This verse indicates that a sure witness of Christ includes the gift of seeing beyond this world. While receiving a witness that we will receive eternal life in the world to come is powerful, the sure witness of Christ while in this life is incomparable. The desired destination of the Journey of Faith is to achieve such faithful conviction that we achieve in mortality what we have seen with the Eye of Faith and felt with the Heart of Faith. In verses 20 and 21, Moroni explains that the brother of Jared had such faith in Christ as to obtain a sure witness of Christ. His faith allowed him to see beyond the veil and obtain a witness of Jesus while still in this life.

Recall that we've seen examples of how faith can help us clear the obstacles that keep us from receiving a more sure witness of Christ. We read that Moroni is aware of the fact that his writings and all of what he and his father had compiled in their book would come forth, and be used to bring souls to Christ: "And it is by faith that my fathers have obtained the promise that these things should come unto their brethren through the Gentiles; therefore the Lord hath commanded me, yea, even Jesus Christ" (Ether 12:22). He understood that the commandment given him to write and compile the records was a fulfillment of the faith of those who had come before. Just imagine what it would feel like to know that you were supposed to write something that would be used at some future date to fulfill the promises the Lord had made to your faithful ancestors.

It appears that Moroni lacked confidence that he had the tools (or perhaps lacked confidence that he was the tool) to do the work the Lord had promised those faithful ancestors, which He asked Moroni to do: "And I said unto him: Lord, the Gentiles will mock at these things, because of our weakness in writing; for Lord thou hast made us mighty in word by faith, but thou hast not made us mighty in writing; for thou hast made all this people that they could speak much, because of the Holy Ghost which thou hast given them; And thou hast made us that we could write but little, because of the awkwardness of our hands. Behold, thou hast not made us mighty in writing like unto the brother of Jared, for thou madest him that the things which he wrote were mighty even as thou art, unto the overpowering of man to read them. Thou hast also made our words powerful and great, even that we cannot write them; wherefore, when we write we behold our weakness, and stumble because of the placing of our words; and I fear lest the Gentiles shall mock at our words" (Ether 12:23–25).

I think a little background on Moroni can help us understand why he felt inadequate to fulfill the Lord's purposes.

Consider that Moroni had read the writings of the brother of Jared and was amazed at the power of his words and his experiences). Moroni's own writing did not feel so powerful to him. And yet, Moroni's words were supposed to give a powerful witness of Christ, and bring us to Him. How could Moroni give the witness he wanted to give when his language felt so inadequate? Their written language was clumsy, he said, and incapable of capturing the power of the words they could speak by the Holy Ghost. Back in Mormon 8:12, he said: "And whoso receiveth this record, and shall not condemn it because of the imperfections which are in it, the same shall know of greater things than these. Behold, I am Moroni; and were it possible, I would make all things known unto you." He also said in that chapter: "Behold, the Lord hath shown unto me great and marvelous things concerning that which must shortly come, at that day when these things shall come forth among you. Behold, I speak unto you as if ye were present, and yet ye are not. But behold, Jesus Christ hath shown you unto me, and I know your doing" (Mormon 8:34–35). He knew what our conditions and problems would be, and he understood enough that he could "make all things known unto" us.

And yet here he was, required to write in a clumsy language that was inadequate to capture the power of the words he felt, incapable of conveying what he knew. That clumsy language was his only tool, and his task was to provide a powerful witness of Christ.

Moroni had a struggle with faith here, because he could not see any path from where he was to the promise which he and others hoped for. The circumstances where we are asked to exercise faith are going to be different from Moroni's, but we may also face uncertainties or hesitations as to how we, being imperfect, can help accomplish the Lord's purposes. We may also be uncertain as to how the Lord is going to be able to fulfill His promises, similar to what we saw with Abraham. That will especially be true when it seems like we need to be something we currently are not. Remember my experience on the treasure hunt? My wife and I inadvertently missed a clue that required the organizers to step in and direct us to the lunch destination—we couldn't get there ourselves because of our mistake. The same can be true of our Journey of Faith. No matter our efforts in life, we'll make mistakes, and miss "clues" or testimonies on the Journey of Faith. Some we'll miss because we'll try to make our own sense out of our experiences. Some we'll miss simply because we'll stray from the path for a time due to our human frailty. However, the Lord's purposes will be fulfilled, as we can learn from the next section of Moroni's example. Let the Lord's reassurance to Moroni be reassurance to you in every Trial of Faith and struggle you experience. Use that reassurance to work through that Trial of Faith to arrive at the next witness in the Journey of Faith.

The Lord spoke to Moroni and told him: "Fools mock, but they shall mourn; and my grace is sufficient for the meek, that they shall take no advantage of your weakness" (Ether 12:26). The Lord reassured Moroni that His grace is sufficient.

We'll only talk about grace a little bit because it is brought up by Moroni with respect to faith. I believe the Lord wanted Moroni, and all of us, to understand that grace is a foundation of faith in Christ. Recall that "if a man have faith he must needs have hope" (Moroni 7:42). Let me suggest that we would not have hope in Christ without knowing that through His grace we can be lifted to a higher state. Let me also suggest that every act of faithfulness we observe on the part of the Lord is evidence of His grace—He blesses us with divine help.

So, we actually gain faith through the grace of Christ. I think that is why we rightly say faith is a gift from God. And it is also a gift that God extends to all of us who will receive it, so any of us can lay hold of it. With that in mind, the Lord continues: "And if men come unto me I will show unto them their weakness. I give unto men weakness that they may be humble; and my grace is sufficient for all men that humble themselves before me; for if they humble themselves before me, and have faith in me, then will I make weak things become strong unto them. Behold, I will show unto the Gentiles their weakness, and I will show unto them that faith, hope and charity bringeth unto me—the fountain of all righteousness" (Ether 12:27–28).

I have heard verse 27 quoted a lot since I was a kid, and it seems that the teaching that is most frequently pointed out is that we can come to the Lord with our weaknesses and ask that He make us stronger. I think that is a beautiful and a powerful teaching from this verse. I also think there is more we can learn. What initially intrigues me about verse 27 is that the Lord says He will show us our weakness if we come unto Him. Most of the applications of this verse that I have heard focus only on taking our weaknesses to the Lord, without pointing out that He says *He will show us* our weakness, meaning that He will show us what weakness we need to focus on. While it is powerful to understand that we can take our weaknesses to the Lord to have Him help us become stronger, to me it is even more powerful to understand that if I come to the Lord He will tell me what I should be working on, and then help me with it.

Remember how we got to this verse in the first place—Moroni encountered his weakness when doing the work the Lord asked him to do. I think of this as the Lord's encouragement for Moroni to continue to act in faith and do what has been asked of him, because he will get the help he needs to accomplish His purposes.

It appears, doesn't it, that the Lord says He gives us weakness that we may be humble? Now wait a second here: I'm already an imperfect being that has plenty to work on. Am I understanding this correctly that God gives us weakness?

I've discussed this with my wife, and we noticed a couple of things that I will share. The first is that it specifically says God "gives" us weakness. When God gives something, it is always a gift; it is always for our benefit. God wants to help us improve and progress (see Moses 1:39). We would do well to remember that everything God gives is a good gift to accomplish His purposes (see Matthew 7:7–11 and Luke 11:9–13). But how can giving us weakness be a gift? It is clearer when looking at the broader context of God giving us the chance to live in mortal weakness and to experience the Trial of Faith. These are His gifts to allow us to progress eternally. They are the gifts necessary to use our agency to come unto God.

He gives us weakness—so that we can humble ourselves and come unto Him. Maybe this verse isn't talking about handing out weaknesses to an already imperfect being, so much as it is talking about giving us the chance to deal with and overcome all weakness to achieve our potential. Remember how the Lord tried Abraham in his Trial of Faith by commanding him to sacrifice his son. The Lord says here that He has grace sufficient for all who humble themselves. Perhaps the gift of weakness is to encourage us to come unto Him as we struggle with our weakness and recognize we need a higher power to help. We'll feel that weakness even as we seek after God, as I believe He will sometimes lead us on a rough path of the Journey of Faith where we will be unable to stand on our own.

As we feel the weight of our burdens on the Journey of Faith, our weakness is exposed. Are there any weaknesses you are aware of in yourself? When are those most clearly apparent? For me, I have done a lot of work to replace my naturally bad temper with patience. However, in times of increased stress and difficulty, that weakness seems to pop out of nowhere to remind me it has not been completely overcome (and honestly, I start to wonder if it ever will be). I also have other private struggles with weaknesses that I've worked on for a long time that might suddenly pop out of nowhere to battle me again. The challenges we face in life can expose our weakness. Perhaps the Lord intends to remind us that we cannot stand on our own, but should be completely reliant on Him in all circumstances.

We will find that even in those challenging times, we can hear His words: "my grace is sufficient for all men that humble themselves before me" (Ether 12:27). The Lord mercifully allows us to struggle against the weight of our burdens so that we can become stronger. And even as we struggle, He takes care of whatever is needed, because His grace is sufficient. Remember those driving winds and waves when talking about the brother of Jared that will drive us to the promised land? The Lord does not intend to cloister us from the challenges and burdens of life. He intends for us to exercise our faith to build strength and become perfected in Him. And in all of this, there is the assurance that if we humble ourselves before the Lord and exercise our faith, God will "make weak things become strong." All of these things are to drive us to God.

Until this point we've only focused on verse 27, but verse 28 extends our understanding and sets up the rest of the chapter: "Behold, I will show unto the Gentiles their weakness, and I will show unto them that faith, hope and charity bringeth unto me—the fountain of all righteousness." From this verse we learn that God will show that faith, hope, and charity will *bring* us unto Him. So if we come unto God, He will show us our weakness, and then we can be humble and exercise faith and have weak things become strong. Exercising true faith should bring us to a witness or testimony of God and His truths. But it is faith mixed with hope and charity that brings us to God, or brings us to all righteousness.

Now let's get back to the specific account at hand—the struggle of Moroni. I am certain that Moroni understood the following two principles: first, that "faith cometh by hearing, and hearing by the word of God" (Romans 10:17). Second, God "prepared a way that thereby others might be partakers of the heavenly gift, that they might hope for those things which they have not seen" (Ether 12:8). So recapping Moroni's struggle, he understood that his writings were to be the fulfillment of both of those principles. But he lamented that his writing was not good enough to capture the power of what he felt, and would instead cause the reader to "mock" at his words. In response to that concern, the Lord gave him the words in verses 26 to 29.

One thing I find very interesting about all of this is that we have no evidence that Moroni was blessed with power to become a better writer after this exchange with the Lord. In fact, instead of finding out that the Lord miraculously blessed him to be better able to communicate his testimony in his writings, we find at the end of Ether 12 that he still laments his "weakness in writing" (verse 40). We might think that Moroni's words do carry power, but they were not sufficient in *his* mind for the task the Lord had given him. And yet, Moroni received comfort in his weakness, and the Lord's assurance that *He* would make Moroni's offering enough through His grace. For me, letting go enough to know that my best effort is not going to be good enough to satisfy myself, and yet offering it anyway so the Lord can use it to perform His work, can certainly be a time when my "nose hits that cold, hard wall." There are times we will simply need to be comforted and come to understand that the Lord accepts what we can offer. Both we and the Lord will understand that our offering is insufficient—but the Lord will make it sufficient to carry out His purposes.

So, in what seems like a twist on the way we normally think of faith, Moroni needed to exercise faith to accept *his own* efforts. He needed to put his trust in God that He could do His own work, whatever it was that Moroni had to offer to it. I find it interesting what Moroni does next to bolster his own faith: he calls on examples from the past, examples of faith, and thoughts of hope and charity to bring himself unto God. Moroni's experience suggests that calling on hope and charity will actually increase our faith more than just working on faith itself. Perhaps that is related to what we've talked about above, that the Journey of Faith is a journey of becoming something. In fact, Moroni's own experience in writing about exercising faith to overcome his obstacles and coming to Christ to receive a witness of Him, is in fact an example of the process of exercising faith to overcome obstacles and come to Christ to receive a witness of Him.

Consider this question: what keeps me from Christ? I can humble myself and find out from Christ what keeps me from Him and then exercise faith to watch the miracles of obstacles being removed. In that process, weak things can be made strong in Christ. We begin to become what we are destined to become as we travel on the Journey of Faith. Even if we don't achieve something to our satisfaction, if we offer what we are to the Lord, and we try to become what He wants us to become, His grace is sufficient for us.

The first thing Moroni does in response to God's words of comfort is to acknowledge that the will of the Lord be done: "And I, Moroni, having heard these words, was comforted, and said: O Lord, thy righteous will be done, for I know that thou workest unto the children of men according to their faith" (Ether 12:29). This is an act of humility, which is exactly what the Lord said is required to make weak things become strong. When we recognize the will of the Lord and submit to it, it means we are willing to do whatever we are asked even though we may not see the wisdom behind it. Perhaps Moroni could not understand why he was supposed to write words to bring people to Christ when someone else had done a better job of it than he could do. And yet, that is what the Lord wanted Moroni to do.

Next Moroni calls on the principle of faith with these words: "For the brother of Jared said unto the mountain Zerin, Remove—and it was removed. And if he had not had faith it would not have moved; wherefore thou workest after men have faith. For thus didst thou manifest thyself unto thy disciples; for after they had faith, and did speak in thy name, thou didst show thyself unto them in great power" (Ether 12:30–31). The first example of faith is to have a mountain removed, which I think is symbolic of the largest obstacle imaginable. This wasn't just prison walls tumbling or feeling the influence of the Holy Spirit—this was a mountain moving! And it moved after the exercise of faith, for that is how God manifests Himself to those who seek Him. The second example of faith is that the

Lord showed Himself to His disciples "in great power," which I think again represents the sure witness of Christ. Moroni keeps coming back to the same themes: removing that which keeps us separated from God, and seeking diligently after a sure witness of Christ.

I think all of these examples lead to a conclusion about faith and how to exercise it, which is one that we may not hear very frequently. We talk about "having faith" in each of the examples where miracles occurred. I think my challenge from childhood has been that I understood all those examples as being situations where people turned on faith like a light switch. But now I think powerful faith takes a long time to develop, like growing the tree of testimony. In fact, I think faith grows in strength in conjunction with the tree of testimony. So, we wouldn't normally come into a situation without faith or unsure of our faith, and suddenly muster a whole lot of faith necessary to have a miracle happen. I just don't think that great faith is like a light switch. Faith is spiritual strength, and like physical strength, it must be developed first with small weights, and later with larger ones; first with gentle resistance, and later with greater resistance. Miracles occur when we come into a situation where more faith is required than we currently have. We put all of our spiritual strength into trusting that God will bring us through or deliver us from our challenges. The miracle is when He does.

I think Moroni was building up his own faith here by humbly calling on these examples of faith. He had humbled himself to recognize that the situation he was in did not make sense to him. And yet, God had the power to remove a mountain when his faithful servant commanded it be done, and He showed Himself with power to those with great faith who were ready to do what He commanded. Moroni knew that

God still had that power. Hopefully you know that God *still has* that power.

Examples of faith in and of themselves can motivate us to action, which can be a very good thing. But calling on the principle of faith naturally leads to hope in Christ, and Moroni's process of building up his spiritual strength doesn't end by reflecting on examples of great faith of others. He reflects on hope so he can contemplate where he was headed with that faith, as he expresses with these words: "And I also remember that thou hast said that thou hast prepared a house for man, yea, even among the mansions of thy Father, in which man might have a more excellent hope; wherefore man must hope, or he cannot receive an inheritance in the place which thou hast prepared" (Ether 12:32). I think calling on the principle of hope can give us perspective.

One of the key things in what Moroni says about hope is that God "prepared" the thing hoped for. It is because God has prepared it for us that we can have a "more excellent hope" in it. When God has prepared it, we don't just try to imagine something in the distance that we anticipate reaching. Instead, we are sure that God has it waiting for us, and we feel more certain that our vision of it is real. Then we become what the Journey of Faith requires of us to get to the hoped-for reward.

Again, Moroni's process of building up his spiritual strength doesn't end by reflecting on hope. He calls on the principle of charity with these words: "And again, I remember that thou hast said that thou hast loved the world, even unto the laying down of thy life for the world, that thou mightest take it again to prepare a place for the children of men. And now I know that this love which thou hast had for the children of men is charity; wherefore, except men shall have charity they cannot inherit that place which thou hast prepared in the mansions of thy Father" (Ether 12:33–34). I believe that

Moroni is saying that charity reminds us that faith is supposed to be making us something. After all, charity is about the heart and what we feel inside, as we become like Christ and develop the capacity to love perfectly as He does. It goes back to the idea that we must become pure, and we must try to be perfect as Jesus is perfect to receive that place prepared for us. Again, this reminds me that getting somewhere with faith occurs only as we become something through faith. And God helps us become something as we come unto Him to make weak things become strong. So getting somewhere with faith requires us to first come unto Christ, who helps us become something, by which we get somewhere through faith.

Next, I think Moroni came to understand that whether or not his writing was weak, his faith was manifested in how he opened his heart to accept the will of the Lord. So Moroni could take comfort in the fact that the Lord would use his words, no matter what he himself thought of them: "Wherefore, I know by this thing which thou hast said, that if the Gentiles have not charity, because of our weakness, that thou wilt prove them, and take away their talent, yea, even that which they have received, and give unto them who shall have more abundantly" (Ether 12:35).

Moroni was initially concerned with his shortcomings, but he concluded that the Lord could work with what Moroni had to offer. The same is true of our efforts in everything that we do to come unto God and diligently serve Him. Our efforts may be inadequate, but from the perspective of seeking to perfect our faith, the spirit in which we act is probably more important than the actual output of our actions. Moroni's test of faith was in putting his words down and allowing the Lord to do the rest. The Journey of Faith is individual, and each of us must individually go through our own test. No one else's work will gain faith for us, nor will the weakness of someone else's work excuse us from seeking after our own faith.

Moroni ends with his personal witness and a challenge for us to obtain our own witness: "And then shall ye know that I have seen Jesus, and that he hath talked with me face to face, and that he told me in plain humility, even as a man telleth another in mine own language, concerning these things. And only a few have I written, because of my weakness in writing. And now, I would commend you to seek this Jesus of whom the prophets and apostles have written, that the grace of God the Father, and also the Lord Jesus Christ, and the Holy Ghost, which beareth record of them, may be and abide in you forever. Amen" (Ether 12:39–41).

Not only does Moroni provide examples of how to overcome the things which keep us from God, he provides a personal example of how to work through our personal doubts and struggles, which will frequently keep us from acting in faith. He was able to remove his obstacles and obtain the object of his faith in Christ.

Where are you on the Journey of Faith? What hope do you have? On the Journey of Faith, we are trying to reach the object of our faith, which may require us to change our perspective as well as our personality. We do not just travel, but change, on the Journey of Faith. We become what we must be to receive what we hope to receive. So how do we start, and how do we move?

Alma provides us the process for growing the power of faith in our lives, from planting the seed of faith to nourishing the tree of testimony. We have reviewed a number of examples and explored a lot of issues that come in that Journey of Faith. But ultimately, whatever we encounter along the path, Alma's process holds true. We must first desire the promised land. We will never take a spiritual step without desiring to walk the path to the promised land. The first step is giving ear to the word of the promise, because faith comes by hearing the word of God. We plant the seed by acting on it to test that it is a good seed, because action moves us along the Journey of Faith. When the seed begins to grow, we act with increased expectation for the expected outcome, because hope drives the Journey of Faith. We feel the swelling and growing of our faith and receive increased light and truth. As we feel that, we understand that God is the rewarder of those who take the journey, which further nourishes our faith. Finally, our faith becomes testimony, and we partake of the fruit our tree bears. We obtain witnesses or testimony all along the Journey of Faith, until we ultimately taste of the fruit of the tree of life and have that sure witness. We then make our testimony and faith a living part of us.

Notes

1. *Lectures on Faith* (1985), 1, 3.
2. Boyd K. Packer, "The Candle of the Lord," *Ensign*, January 1983.
3. See *Lectures on Faith* (1985), 3.

LIVING FAITH

Despite how deeply we've looked at some things, let me emphasize that I don't want to make faith sound complicated. At its core, faith is really very simple: it is about trust and action. We act because we trust. We act so we can be trusted. Those simple relationships explain the two-way street of trust that characterizes something we'll now refer to as Living Faith. Let's also add one more piece: we trust because we have acted and observed the outcome. The key is making that Leap of Faith to get into the cycle of trust and action. Faith is about a series of faith-acts, and it comes alive as we make our first trust-act. That is how we start the Journey of Faith. Living Faith is the true faith that we exercise on the Journey of Faith. Living Faith is the source of strength that will help us through the Trial of Faith. Living Faith is what brings us to the Light and dispels darkness.

Living Faith is the real faith we've been discussing from the beginning of this book. Living Faith is identified in individuals who have built up conviction and peace. Recall that we can have faith in ourselves, in our own abilities, in other people, or in other things. In all instances of real faith that I can think of, the individual possessing faith builds up conviction in, and peace with respect to, the object of their faith. But when we refer to Living Faith, we're referring to real faith in Jesus Christ. It is an external manifestation of our conviction to Jesus Christ and His Gospel and internal peace with respect to our relationship with Him. The "four C's" we discussed earlier—conviction, change, commitment, and courage—make faith alive, as we are committed to adopting the change necessary to overcome whatever keeps us separated from God.

Notice that the expression *Living Faith* can be read as having one of two different meanings, both of which apply to the real faith we've been discussing. In the first meaning, the word *living* can be understood as a verb. Thus, *Living Faith* connotes that true faith is expressed in how we live. When we embody true faith, we will be living *our* faith. In the second meaning, the word *living* can be understood as an adjective modifying the word *faith*. Thus, *Living Faith* connotes that true faith itself is alive. This reminds us that as we nourish faith, it will grow, because it is a living thing. Conversely, it can wither away by neglect or abuse. Living Faith in this sense can also be understood to provide something to us—to give life to our actions. These two concepts, with *Living* as either a verb or an adjective, really go together. As we live our faith, we will generate faith that is alive and life-giving. If we want to make our faith true, it will necessarily require us to root our seed of faith in true principles and get out and live it by acting on our faith. Then it will grow into a Tree of Life or the tree of testimony that bears fruit.

ABOUT *the* AUTHOR

Vincent Anderson is married to Mayel Anderson and has four daughters. They live in Marin County, California. Vincent is a practicing patent attorney and a lifelong student of the scriptures. Vincent graduated from Brigham Young University with a bachelor's degree in electrical engineering before moving to Oregon to attend Willamette University College of Law.

Scan to visit

www.vincentandersonauthor.com